Learn to Decorate
Cupcakes and
Other Bakes

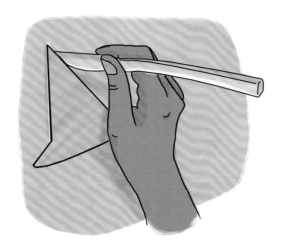

4 Lay one hat template on the dough and carefully cut around it with a round-bladed knife. Cut the next as close to it as possible. When you need to, gather the dough scraps together, and roll it out again. Keep cutting hats but you could always use some of the dough to stamp out some simple cookie shapes.

5 Lay all the cookies on the lined baking trays and ask an adult to put them into the preheated oven for 12–16 minutes until the cookies are golden.

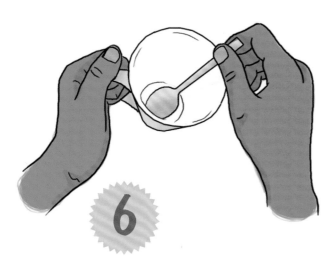

6 Make a little "edible glue" by putting two tablespoons of confectioner's (icing) sugar in a cup and adding two tablespoons of warm water. Stir them together.

7 Tint the white fondant purple either using purple paste or mixing your own purple with blue and red coloring liquids (see page 21). To mix a purple, put 10 drops of red and 5 drops of blue in a bowl and stir together. Add a drop more red to lighten it, or blue to darken it.

8

Sprinkle a little confectioner's (icing) sugar onto a clean work surface. Roll out the black fondant icing until it is about ¼ in. (5 mm) thick. Each time you roll the icing, lift it, turn it a little, and sprinkle on a little more confectioner's sugar to stop it sticking to the work surface. Sprinkle a little sugar on the rolling pin too, if that sticks.

9

Using the cardboard templates, cut out icing hats to match the cookies.

10

Brush a little of your "sugar glue" onto the cookies and stick on the icing hats.

11

Roll out some purple icing so it is very thin. Cut some thin strips and attach them around the bottom of each witch's hat as a trim using your "glue" to stick them down. Decorate the hats using the writing icing.

Gingerbread family

Everyone has read the story of the gingerbread man, but why stop with a gingerbread man—you can make gingerbread women and children, too! Make a whole gingerbread family and dress them in clothes made from icing and candies.

You will need:

1 quantity Gingerbread dough (see page 17)

all-purpose (plain) flour, for rolling out

writing icing

colored candy-coated chocolate drops

other decorations like currants, cashew nuts, silver balls

gingerbread people cutters in assorted sizes

2 baking trays

nonstick baking parchment

(makes 10–12)

1 Ask an adult to help you make the Gingerbread dough (see page 17). When the dough is well chilled, turn the oven on to 325°F (170°C) Gas 3. Cut pieces of nonstick baking parchment to cover the baking trays.

2 Lightly dust a clean, dry surface with flour and roll out the dough to a thickness of ¼ in. (5 mm). Use the cutters to stamp out as many people as possible from the dough, cutting each one as close as possible to the next one. Arrange the people on the baking trays.

3 Gather the dough scraps together, knead lightly, re-roll, and stamp out more people until all the dough has been used up.

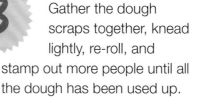

4 Ask an adult to help you bake the gingerbread in batches on the middle shelf of the preheated oven for 10–12 minutes or until it is firm and lightly browned at the edges. Allow the cookies to cool completely on the baking trays before you ice them.

5 Use writing icing to draw faces and clothes on each person. You can decorate yours with more colors than we did and use currants, silver balls, and nuts, as well as candy-coated chocolate drops, to make the faces and clothes or buttons. Stick on the candies and other decorations with small blobs of writing icing.

RUN, RUN, as fast as you can, you can't catch me—
I'm the GINGERBREAD MAN!

Snowy village

Make fairy-tale gingerbread houses like the one in the story of Hansel and Gretel. The magical stained glass windows are made with hard, clear candies, which melt in the oven.

You will need:

1 quantity Gingerbread dough (see page 17)

all-purpose (plain) flour, for rolling out

4 oz. (125 g) clear, hard, fruit candies

writing icing

stiff card to make templates (cereal packets work well)

baking trays

nonstick baking parchment

(makes 6–10 houses)

1

Ask an adult to help you make the Gingerbread dough (see page 17). While the gingerbread dough is chilling, make the templates for the houses. Draw 3 houses, all different shapes and sizes, onto pieces of card and cut them out. The largest should be no bigger than about 8–12 in. (20–30 cm) high or wide. Smaller ones are less likely to break.

2 Turn the oven on to 325°F (170°C) Gas 3. Cut pieces of nonstick baking parchment to cover the baking trays.

3 Lightly dust a clean, dry work surface with flour. Divide the dough into 3 pieces. Have a big piece for a big house and a smaller piece for a smaller house. Roll the biggest piece of dough out to about ¼ in. (5 mm) thick and lay the biggest house template on top. Carefully cut around it using a round-bladed knife. Slide the gingerbread house onto the baking tray. Cut out the other two houses in the same way.

4

Using a small, sharp knife or cookie cutters, carefully cut out windows from each house.

5 Unwrap the hard fruit candies, divide them into separate colors and place each color in its own freezer bag. Using a rolling pin, crush the candies into small pieces and then pour each color into a separate bowl. Put to one side.

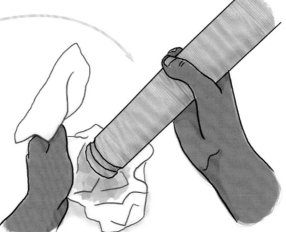

WHO LIVES in YOUR gingerbread house?

6 Ask an adult to help you bake the houses on the middle shelf of the preheated oven for about 5 minutes until the gingerbread is just starting to color at the edges. Remove the baking trays from the oven.

7 Carefully and neatly fill the windows in the houses with the crushed fruit candies. Use a dry pastry brush to brush away any stray candy pieces. Return the baking trays to the oven and bake for a further 5 minutes until the gingerbread is golden brown and firm and the candies have melted to fill the window shapes. Be careful not to bake them for too long—if the candies start to bubble they could lose their color. Allow the houses to cool completely on the baking trays.

Learn to Decorate Cupcakes and Other Bakes

35 recipes for making and decorating cupcakes, brownies, and cookies

CICO kidz

This edition published in 2022 by CICO Books
An imprint of Ryland Peters & Small
20–21 Jockey's Fields   341 E 116th St
London WC1R 4BW   New York, NY 10029

First published in 2012 as
My First Cupcake Decorating Book

www.rylandpeters.com

10 9 8 7 6 5 4 3 2 1

FSC
MIX
Paper from
responsible sources
FSC® C008047

A CIP catalog record for this book is
available from the Library of Congress
and the British Library.

ISBN: 978 1 80065 152 4

Printed in China

Series consultant: Susan Akass
Editors: Susan Akass, Katie Hardwicke
Designers: Elizabeth Healey, Barbara Zuniga
Step artworks: Rachel Boulton
Animal artworks: Hannah George
For photography credits, see page 128.

Art director: Sally Powell
Production manager: Gordana Simakovic
Publishing manager: Penny Craig
Publisher: Cindy Richards

All spoon measurements are level unless
otherwise specified.

Both imperial and metric measurements have
been given. Use one set of measurements
only and not a mixture of both.

All eggs are US large (UK medium) unless
otherwise stated. This book contains recipes
made with raw eggs. It is prudent for more
vulnerable people, such as pregnant and
nursing mothers, babies and young children,
invalids and the elderly, to avoid uncooked
dishes made with eggs.

Some of the recipes contain nuts and should
not be consumed by anyone with a nut allergy.

Ovens should be preheated to the specified
temperatures. All ovens work slightly
differently. We recommend using an oven
thermometer and suggest you consult the
maker's handbook for any special instructions,
particularly if you are cooking in a fan-assisted
oven, as you will need to adjust temperatures
according to manufacturer's instructions.

Contents

Introduction	6
Kitchen safety and basic equipment	7
Cupcakes	8
Basic cake pops	12
Brownies	14
Vanilla cookie dough	16
Gingerbread dough	17
Frostings and icings	18
Tinting icing	21
Other techniques	22

CHAPTER ONE: COOL CUPCAKES 24

Easter bunny cupcakes	26
Mini strawberry cakes	30
Crystallized pansies	32
Spotty cupcakes	35
A rainbow of cupcakes	38
Christmas stockings	40
Butterfly cakes	42
Special name cupcakes	44
Sparkling diamond cupcakes	47
Pink piggy cupcakes	50
Victoria cupcakes	54
Princess cupcakes	56
Animal-face cupcakes	58
Chocolate and jelly bean cupcakes	62
"Ice cream" cupcakes	64
Snowmen in scarves	66

CHAPTER TWO: CAKE POPS 70

Sprinkle pops and swirly pops	72
Sailboat pops	74
Goldfish pops	76
Butterfly pops	78
Alien pops	81
Sheep pops	84
Flower pops	86

CHAPTER THREE: BROWNIES, COOKIES, AND GINGERBREAD 88

Stenciled brownies	90
Rocky roadies	92
Brownie owls	94
Brownie pops	97
Marbled cheesecake brownies	100
Stained glass window cookies	103
Ladybug cookies	106
Christmas tree cookies	111
Witches and wizards	114
Gingerbread family	118
Snowy village	120
Gingerbread animals	124

Templates	126
Suppliers	127
Index and acknowledgments	128

Introduction

Cupcakes look fabulous, taste delicious, and are fun and easy to make. In this book, we have a whole bunch of exciting ways to decorate a cupcake. But why stop at cupcakes? The latest trend is cake pops—yummy, creamy cakes on a stick—and we have a chapter on how to make and decorate these little beauties. Finally, there is a chapter of scrumptious chocolate brownies, gingerbread, and cookies to be made and decorated in a stunning variety of different ways.

Before you decorate, you need to bake your cakes or cookies, and we have included recipes and detailed instructions on how to do this. Of course, you will always need to ask an adult's permission before you start, and will need to ask for help with heating ingredients on the stove and using the oven, but, as you become more experienced, you will be able to do more and more of the cooking yourself. The decorating is the really exciting part and you can do most of this by yourself or, for even more fun, with the help of a friend. What better way of spending an afternoon than creating stunning cakes for your birthday tea, or a special picnic, or a sleepover?

Most of the recipes use ingredients which you will probably have at home or which you can buy at the supermarket. A few use more specialist ingredients, which you can buy online or at specialist stores.

To help you, we have graded all the projects with one, two, or three smiley faces. The grade one projects are easy and can be made with ingredients from the supermarket. Grade two projects are a little trickier, take more time and patience, and may use some specialist ingredients. Grade three projects also use specialist ingredients and are the hardest. They include more difficult techniques, such as using an icing bag.

Happy baking!

Project levels

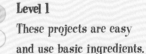 **Level 1**
These projects are easy and use basic ingredients.

Level 2
These projects are a little harder and may use specialist ingredients.

 Level 3
These projects use more advanced techniques and specialist ingredients.

Kitchen safety—read this before you start cooking!

- Always wash your hands before you start cooking.

- Tie long hair back so that it is out of the way.

- Wear an apron to keep your clothes clean.

- Make sure your ingredients are fresh and within their use-by date.

- When using sharp knives, electrical equipment, or the stove, microwave, or oven, always ask an adult to help you.

- Use oven gloves when holding hot pans or dishes.

- When using the stove, make sure that saucepan handles don't stick out over the front of the hob where you could knock them off.

- Always remember to turn off the heat when you've finished cooking.

- Use a chopping board when using a sharp knife or metal cookie cutters —this protects the work surface and will help to stop the knife from slipping.

- Keep your work surface clean and wipe up any spills on the floor so that you don't slip.

- Don't forget to clear up afterward—washing the dishes can be as much fun as baking!

Basic equipment

Mixing bowls in different sizes

Heatproof glass bowls

Microwave-safe bowls

Wooden spoon

Measuring pitcher (jug)

Weighing scales or measuring cups

Wire whisk

Spatula

Pastry brush

Rolling pin

Strainer (sieve)

Measuring spoons

12-hole muffin pans

12-hole mini muffin pan

Baking trays

Cake pans

Small saucepan

Cookie cutters

Grater

Lemon squeezer

Baking parchment

Sharp knives

Palette knife

Wire cooling rack

Paper cupcake cases

Mini muffin cases

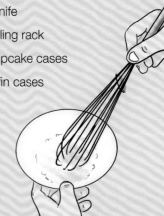

Basic Recipes

Vanilla cupcakes

You will need:

¾ cup (175 g) unsalted butter, softened

1 cup (175 g) superfine (caster) sugar

3 eggs

1 teaspoon vanilla extract

1¾ cup (175 g) all-purpose (plain) flour

3 teaspoons baking powder

3 tablespoons milk

12-hole muffin pan

paper cupcake cases

(makes about 12)

 1 Ask an adult to turn the oven on to 350°F (180°C) Gas 4.

2 Line the muffin pan with paper cupcake cases.

3 Put the soft butter and sugar in a large mixing bowl and beat with a wooden spoon until the butter is soft, creamy, and pale (if an adult is helping, you could use an electric beater).

4 Break the eggs into a small bowl and remove any pieces of shell. Beat the eggs with a fork until the yolks have broken up and the mixture is bit frothy.

5 Add a little egg to the creamed butter mixture and beat with the wooden spoon until the egg is all blended in. Then add a little more egg and beat again. Add a small sprinkle of flour if the mixture looks as though it is starting to separate (becoming bitty rather than smooth). Keep adding the egg until it is all used up and scrape any mixture down from the sides with a spatula.

6 Add the vanilla extract and stir it into the mixture.

7 Sift the flour and baking powder together into a separate bowl.

8 Add the flour to the mixture in two halves. Fold the first half gently into the mixture with a big metal spoon. Don't beat or over-stir it—gentle folding traps air into the mixture and will make the cakes lovely and light. When this is mixed in, add the second half and do the same.

9 Carefully spoon the cake mixture into the paper cases in the muffin pan. Put the same amount into each one, so they are about two-thirds full.

10 Ask an adult to help you put the cakes in the oven and bake them for 15–20 minutes until they are risen and golden and the cakes are springy to touch.

11 Ask an adult to help you take the pan out of the oven and let it cool a little. Then lift out the cakes and put them on a wire rack to cool down while you make the frosting.

12 Decorate your cupcakes following the recipe and store in an airtight container for up to 4 days.

Chocolate cupcakes

You will need:

1¼ cups (125 g) all-purpose (plain) flour

1 teaspoon baking powder

a pinch of salt

¼ cup (25 g) cocoa powder

¾ cup (150 g) superfine (caster) sugar

7 tablespoons (100 g) unsalted butter, very soft

2 large eggs

½ cup (125 ml) milk

12-hole muffin pan

paper cupcake cases

(makes about 12)

1 Ask an adult to turn the oven on to 350°F (180°C) Gas 4.

2 Line the muffin pan with paper cupcake cases.

3 Place a large strainer (sieve) over a mixing bowl. Tip the flour, baking powder, salt, cocoa powder, and sugar into the strainer as you measure them, then sift them all into the bowl.

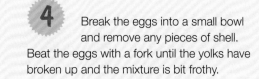

4 Break the eggs into a small bowl and remove any pieces of shell. Beat the eggs with a fork until the yolks have broken up and the mixture is bit frothy.

5   Add the very soft butter to the mixing bowl, along with the eggs and milk. Use a wooden spoon to mix all the ingredients together to make a smooth batter. (If an adult is helping, you could use an electric beater.)

6   Carefully spoon the cake mixture into the paper cases in the muffin pan. Put the same amount into each one, so they are about two-thirds full.

7   Ask an adult to help you put the muffin pan in the oven and bake for 20 minutes, until the cupcakes are risen and just firm to the touch.

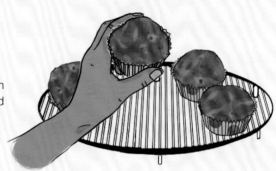

8   Ask an adult to help you remove the pan from the oven and let it cool for 5 minutes. Then lift out the cakes and put them on a wire rack to cool completely while you make the frosting.

9   Decorate your cupcakes following your recipe and store them in an airtight container for up to 4 days.

Basic cake pops

You will need:

4 tablespoons (50 g) unsalted butter, softened

¼ cup (50 g) superfine (caster) sugar

1 egg

1 teaspoon vanilla extract

½ cup (50 g) self-rising (self-raising) flour

2 oz. (50 g) white chocolate, chopped

¼ cup (60 g) cream cheese

8-in (20-cm) square cake pan

baking parchment

(makes 20 pops)

 Ask an adult to turn the oven on to 350°F (180°C) Gas 4.

 Place the baking pan on the baking parchment and draw around it with a pencil. Cut out the square and set it to one side.

 Grease the baking pan by using a piece of kitchen paper and a smear of butter to wipe round the whole of the inside. Now put the square of parchment inside the baking pan. This will stop the cake sticking to the pan.

4 Put the soft butter and sugar in a large mixing bowl and beat with a wooden spoon until the butter is soft, creamy, and pale (if an adult is helping, you could use an electric beater).

 Break one egg into a cup. Take out any bits of shell that might have got into the cup and then tip the egg into the butter and sugar mixture and beat them together.

6 Add the vanilla extract and stir it into the mixture.

7 Put a strainer (sieve) over the bowl. Tip in the flour and sift it into the mixture. Stir everything together until the flour has been mixed in.

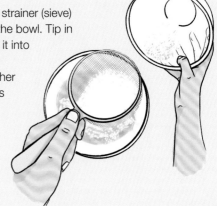

8 Pour the batter into the cake pan.

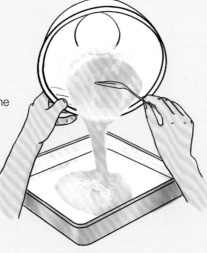

9 Ask an adult to help you put the cake pan on the middle shelf of the preheated oven and bake for 12–15 minutes until golden brown. Leave the cake to cool in the pan.

10 When the cake is cool, crumble it into very small pieces using your fingertips or you can blitz it in a food processor if you have an adult to help you. Put the cake crumbs in a large mixing bowl.

11 Ask an adult to help you melt the white chocolate in a heatproof bowl, either over a pan of simmering water or in the microwave (see page 23). Add the melted white chocolate and cream cheese to the cake crumbs and mix them together with a spoon.

12 Shape the mixture into 20 small balls about the size of a large marble, or as instructed in your recipe. Put the balls on a tray and chill them in the freezer for 30 minutes.

13 Your cake pops are now ready to decorate. Undecorated pops will keep for 4 weeks in the freezer in a sealed container. Decorated cake pops should be kept in the fridge and eaten within 3 days.

Brownies

You will need:

1 cup (100 g) shelled walnuts or pecans (optional)

6½ oz. (200 g) bittersweet (dark) chocolate, chopped

1 stick (125 g) unsalted butter, diced

1¼ cups (250 g) superfine (caster) sugar

4 eggs

1 teaspoon vanilla extract

1¼ cups (125 g) all-purpose (plain) flour

2 tablespoons cocoa powder

a pinch of salt

½ cup (75 g) milk chocolate chips

8 x 12-in. (20 x 30-cm) baking pan

baking parchment

1 Ask an adult to turn the oven on to 325ºF (170ºC) Gas 3.

2 Place the baking pan on the baking parchment and draw around it with a pencil. Cut out the rectangle and set it to one side.

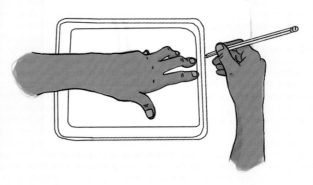

3 Grease the baking pan by using a piece of kitchen paper and a smear of butter to wipe round the whole of the inside. Now put the rectangle of parchment inside the baking pan. This will stop the brownies sticking to the pan.

4 If you would like to use nuts, tip them onto a baking tray and ask an adult to help you lightly toast them in the hot oven for 5 minutes. Let them cool, and then ask an adult to help you chop them. Leave the oven on.

5 Ask an adult to help you with this stage too. Put the chocolate and butter in a heatproof bowl and set it over a saucepan of barely simmering water, or melt them in the microwave (see page 23). Stir them until the butter and chocolate are smooth and mixed together. Let the mixture cool slightly.

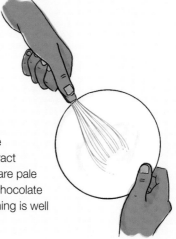

6 In a separate bowl, beat the sugar, eggs, and vanilla extract with a wire whisk until they are pale and thick. Add the melted chocolate mixture and stir until everything is well mixed together.

7 Place a strainer (sieve) over the bowl. Measure the flour, cocoa, and salt into the strainer and sift them into the bowl.

8 Fold in the flour, cocoa, and salt with a big metal spoon until everything is well mixed together, then stir in the chocolate chips and nuts (if you are using them).

9 Pour the mixture into the baking pan, spread it level, and ask an adult to help you put it on the middle shelf of the preheated oven and bake for 25 minutes.

10 Ask an adult to help you remove the brownies from the oven and let them cool completely in the pan. Follow the instructions in your recipe to decorate the brownies. You can store them in an airtight container for up to 4 days.

1 Place a large strainer (sieve) over a mixing bowl. Tip the flours and salt into the strainer and then sift them into the mixing bowl. Put the bowl to one side.

Vanilla cookie dough

You will need:

2½ cups (250 g) all-purpose (plain) flour

1¼ cups (125 g) self-rising (self-raising) flour

pinch of salt

2 sticks (250 g) unsalted butter, at room temperature

⅔ cup (125 g) unrefined superfine (golden caster) sugar

1 large egg

1 teaspoon vanilla extract

2 Put the soft butter and sugar in a large mixing bowl and beat them together with a wooden spoon until the mixture is soft, creamy, and pale (if an adult is helping, you could use an electric beater).

3 Carefully break the egg onto a plate and use an egg cup to separate the yolk from the white (see page 22). You do not need the white for this recipe.

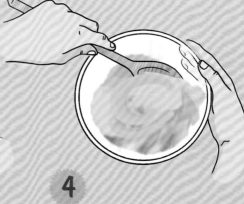

4 Add the egg yolk and vanilla extract to the creamed butter mixture and mix together well.

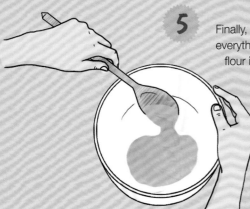

5 Finally, add the flours and mix everything together until all the flour is mixed in and the mixture forms a dough. Stop mixing as soon as the flour is all mixed in.

6 Put the dough in a sealable food bag, or wrap it in plastic wrap (clingfilm), and chill in the refrigerator for 1–2 hours. You are now ready to roll out the dough and follow your recipe.

Gingerbread dough

You will need:
----

2 tablespoons light corn (golden) syrup

1 large egg

2 cups (200 g) all-purpose (plain) flour, plus extra for dusting

½ teaspoon baking powder

1½ teaspoons ground ginger

1 teaspoon ground cinnamon

¼ teaspoon ground nutmeg

a pinch of salt

7 tablespoons (100 g) unsalted butter, chilled and diced

⅓ cup (75 g) light muscovado or light brown (soft) sugar

1 Carefully break the egg onto a plate and use an egg cup to separate the yolk from the white (see page 22). You do not need the white for this recipe.

2 Put the light corn (golden) syrup and egg yolk in a small bowl and beat them together with a wooden spoon.

3 Place a large strainer (sieve) over a mixing bowl. Tip the flour, baking powder, spices, and salt into the strainer and sift them into the bowl.

4 Add the butter and then pick up small amounts of butter and flour and rub them together between your thumb and fingertips. Keep picking up more of the mixture and rubbing it together. In this way, the butter gradually gets mixed into the flour.

5 When the mixture starts to look like sand and there are no lumps of butter, add the sugar and mix it in with your fingers.

Turn OVER for the REST OF THE STEPS!

6 Now add the egg yolk and syrup mixture and mix it with a wooden spoon until the dough starts to clump together.

7 Sprinkle a little flour on your work surface and tip the mixture on top. Knead it gently to form the dough into a smooth ball.

8 Flatten the dough into a disc, put it in a sealable food bag, or wrap it in plastic wrap (clingfilm), and chill it in the refrigerator for 1–2 hours. You are now ready to roll out the dough and follow your recipe.

Frostings and icings

Buttercream frosting

You will need:

----

1 stick (125 g) butter, softened

1 tablespoon milk

3 cups (375 g) confectioner's (icing) sugar

1 Put the butter in a mixing bowl. Add the milk.

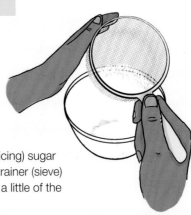

2 Measure the confectioner's (icing) sugar into another bowl. Place a strainer (sieve) over the butter bowl and sift a little of the sugar into the bowl.

3 Remove the sieve and beat the mixture together. Then sift in a little more sugar and beat again. Keep going until all the sugar has been mixed in and the frosting is light, fluffy, and smooth.

4 If you would like to color your frosting, add a little food coloring paste or a couple of drops of liquid food coloring to the mix (see page 21) and stir it in well to get an even color.

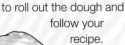

Flavorings

To make your frosting even more special, you can add different flavors.

Lemon or orange buttercream: Use a grater to grate the rind of a lemon or orange onto a small plate.

Cut the orange or lemon in half and use a lemon squeezer to squeeze out the juice. Fish out any pips.

Make the frosting as in the buttercream frosting recipe on page 18, but instead of using milk, use the fresh juice and add the grated rind to the mixture.

Chocolate buttercream: In a cup, mix the milk and 2 tablespoons cocoa powder to a smooth paste and stir it into one quantity of buttercream frosting.

Vanilla buttercream: Add 1 teaspoon of vanilla extract to one quantity of buttercream frosting.

Coffee buttercream: In a cup, mix the milk and 1 tablespoon instant coffee powder to a paste and add to the buttercream frosting.

Fondant icing

Buy fondant icing ready made from supermarkets, cake decorating stores, or websites. White fondant icing can be found at supermarkets and you can tint it to the color you need. Ready-colored fondant icing can be bought from larger supermarkets and specialist stores. Ready-colored is best for really bright or dark colors as it is difficult to tint icing evenly for these.

1 Place a strainer (sieve) over a bowl and sift the confectioner's (icing) sugar into the bowl. Add 2–4 tablespoons of warm water, mixing them quickly until the icing is quite runny, like thin cream. For a thicker icing, add the water a little at a time, until you get the right consistency.

You will need:

----

2 cups (250 g) confectioner's (icing) sugar

2 If you're adding food coloring paste or liquid, add just a little at a time and mix it in well until the color is even and there are no streaks (see page 21).

3 Pour the icing onto your cupcakes or cookies before it starts to set.

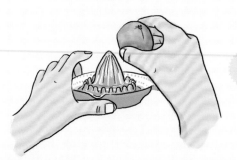

4 To make a really zingy sugar icing, replace the water with freshly squeezed lemon, lime, or orange juice.

Milk chocolate frosting

You will need:

----

4 oz. (125 g) bittersweet (dark) chocolate

4 oz. (125 g) milk chocolate

⅔ cup (175 ml) heavy (double) cream

1 tablespoon maple syrup or light corn syrup (golden syrup)

1 stick (125 g) soft butter, diced

1 Ask an adult to help you chop all the chocolate into small pieces. Put them into a small, heatproof bowl.

2 Ask an adult to help you heat the cream and syrup in a small saucepan until it is just boiling.

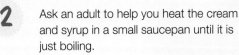

3 Pour the hot cream mixture over the chocolate, add the butter, and let them melt. Stir them together until they are smooth, then let the frosting thicken slightly before you use it.

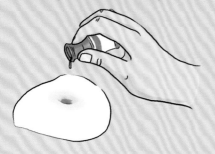

Tinting icing

Whether you are tinting frosting, fondant, or sugar icing, it is best to color it in one batch, otherwise you may end up with different shades. Food coloring pastes or gels are available from specialty cake decorating stores and come in lots of gorgeous colors. They are very strong so a little paste goes a long way. Liquid food coloring is available from supermarkets. You only need to add a few drops at a time to your icing—be very careful not to pour more than that in, as the color will be too strong and the liquid will turn your icing sticky or runny. Marzipan can be colored in the same way.

Tinting fondant icing

1 Push your finger into the fondant to make a small hole. Use a wooden skewer or toothpick to add tiny amounts of food coloring paste or carefully add one or two drops at a time of liquid food coloring to the fondant icing.

2 Knead the fondant so that the color is evenly mixed without any streaks.
 If you want the color to be deeper, add a little more coloring and knead again. Keep doing this until you have the color you want.

Tinting sugar icing and buttercream frosting

Use a wooden skewer or toothpick to add tiny amounts of food coloring paste or add just a drop or two of liquid food coloring to the frosting or icing and mix it in thoroughly with a spoon. If you want the color to be deeper, add a little more coloring and stir again. Keep doing this until you have the color you want.

Mixing colors

It is possible to make different colors by mixing food coloring liquids. Mix the color in a separate bowl before adding it to your icing and test the color first to check that you have the right shade. Here are a few color combinations:

 Red + blue = purple

 Red + green = brown

 Red + yellow = orange

 Blue + yellow = green

Other techniques

Breaking eggs

Firmly tap the egg shell on the side of a bowl or plate and then pull the two halves apart with your fingertips. If any pieces of shell fall into your mixture, scoop them out with a spoon before they are mixed in.

Separating eggs

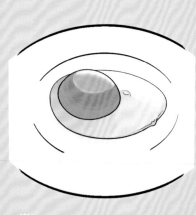

1 To separate the egg yolk from the white, break an egg onto a small plate, keeping the yolk whole.

2 Put an egg cup over the yolk and, holding the plate over a bowl, tip the plate so that the egg white slides off.

Warming jelly and jam

Some recipes ask you to warm jelly or jam to loosen it a little so that it is easier to spread. You can do this in two ways:

On the stove
Ask an adult to help you put the jelly in a saucepan and heat it gently on the stove over a low heat. Take care when stirring as the edges may catch and spit.

Stir with a wooden spoon until the jelly has just warmed through and is runnier.

In the microwave
Put the jelly in a microwave-safe bowl and heat on medium for 20–30 seconds. Ask an adult to help you take the bowl out of the microwave and stir it gently. You can heat again for a few seconds longer if necessary, but take care that the jelly doesn't overheat—jelly can become burning hot very quickly.

Melting chocolate

On the stove

1 Fill a small saucepan a quarter full with water and ask an adult to help you set it on the stove to heat to a gentle simmer (until the water starts to bubble). Turn the heat to low.

2 Put the chopped chocolate in a heatproof bowl that fits in the saucepan and carefully put it in the pan of just simmering water, making sure that the bottom of the bowl doesn't touch the water.

3 Allow the chocolate to melt a little before stirring and when there are just a few small lumps left, remove the bowl from the saucepan and stir until the chocolate is smooth and lump-free.

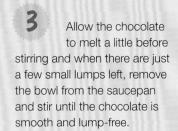

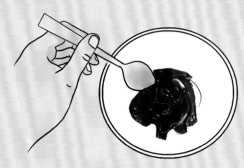

In the microwave

Put the chopped chocolate in a microwave-safe bowl. Heat on low for 30 seconds, stir, and heat again for a further 30 seconds. Keep checking and stirring at regular intervals of 20–30 seconds, and when the chocolate is nearly melted (when there are a few lumps left), remove the bowl from the microwave and stir the melted chocolate until it is smooth. Take care if the bowl is hot and ask an adult to help you take the bowl in and out of the microwave. Take care that the chocolate doesn't overheat.

Microwave safety

- Always use microwave-safe bowls and never put anything metallic in the microwave.
- When heating anything in the microwave you must take great care to stir the heated ingredient thoroughly before using or eating it—even if it seems lukewarm on the outside, it could be burning hot inside. When you stir melted chocolate or jelly (jam), for example, you will spread the heat evenly and avoid these hot spots. Heat on a medium or low setting for short lengths of time rather than continuously, and keep checking at regular intervals.
- These are general instructions as microwave ovens vary, so adapt the timings to suit your particular model.

COOL CUPCAKES

Easter bunny cupcakes	26
Mini strawberry cakes	30
Crystallized pansies	32
Spotty cupcakes	35
A rainbow of cupcakes	38
Christmas stockings	40
Butterfly cakes	42
Special name cupcakes	44
Sparkling diamond cupcakes	47
Pink piggy cupcakes	50
Victoria cupcakes	54
Princess cupcakes	56
Animal-face cupcakes	58
Chocolate and jelly bean cupcakes	62
"Ice cream" cupcakes	64
Snowmen in scarves	66

Easter bunny cupcakes

Making decorations with marzipan is just like using playdough and is lots of fun. These adorable little marzipan rabbits and carrots are the perfect decoration for cupcakes at Easter but you could use your imagination to make all sorts of other animal decorations in a similar way. You will need to make them a day before you make the cupcakes so that the color doesn't run into the cake frosting.

You will need:

10 oz. (300 g) natural marzipan

orange and brown food coloring paste or yellow, red, and green food coloring

white mini-marshmallows

white sugar strands

1 quantity Vanilla cupcake mix (see page 8)

1 quantity Buttercream frosting (see page 18), flavored if you like (see page 19)

angelica

cocoa powder, for sprinkling

airtight container lined with baking parchment

wooden skewer

12-hole muffin pan, lined with paper cupcake cases

(makes 12)

1 Make the marzipan decorations the day before you make the cupcakes so the colors have time to dry. First, find an airtight box to keep your rabbits and carrots in overnight. Cut a piece of baking parchment to fit at the bottom of the box.

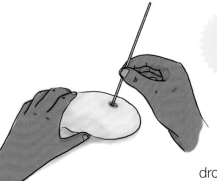

2 Now tint two-thirds of the marzipan orange using the orange food coloring paste (see page 21). Add the paste a little at a time until the marzipan is a nice carroty orange. If you are using the liquids, mix a few drops of red with a few drops of yellow to make orange (see page 21). Make a hole with your finger in the marzipan and drop in a couple of drops of liquid. Knead the marzipan until the color spreads through it. Gradually add more coloring until you have the orange color you want.

3

Tint the rest of the marzipan brown either using the brown food coloring paste or mixing a few drops of red and green food coloring to make brown.

4

To make the carrots, break off small nuggets of orange marzipan and roll them between your hands to make carrot shapes. Three per cake look good but you don't have to make so many.

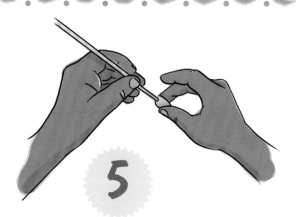

5

Using the blunt end of a wooden skewer, push a small hole into the top of each carrot. This is where you will add the angelica for the carrot leaves. Put the carrots carefully into the container so they don't touch each other.

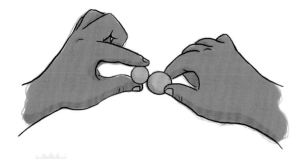

6

Now make a rabbit. Break off a small nugget of brown marzipan and roll it into a ball between your hands for the rabbit's body. Make a smaller ball for the head. Carefully press the head onto the body.

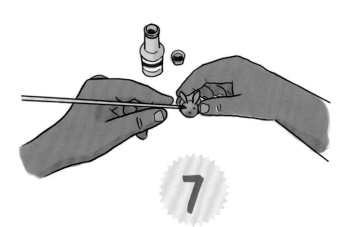

7

Make tiny ears and press them onto the rabbit's head. Dip the point of a wooden skewer or toothpick into the brown food coloring paste or liquid and paint eyes and a nose onto the rabbit.

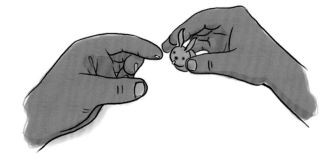

8

Use two white sugar strands and push them into the head, underneath the nose, to make the rabbit's teeth.

9

Press on a mini-marshmallow for a fluffy tail.

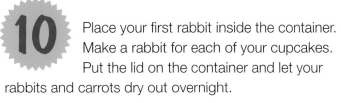

10

Place your first rabbit inside the container. Make a rabbit for each of your cupcakes. Put the lid on the container and let your rabbits and carrots dry out overnight.

11

The next day, cut the angelica into very fine strips about ½ in. (1 cm) long. You will need a sharp knife for this so ask an adult to help you. Push two of the strips into the small hole in the top of each carrot.

12

Ask an adult to help you make the cupcakes (see page 8). While they are cooling make the buttercream frosting, adding some flavoring if you like (see page 18). Once the cakes are cold, spread the frosting over the top of each cupcake. Sprinkle a little cocoa powder over the icing and decorate each cupcake with a rabbit and some carrots.

Easter bunnies for **EASTER** *cupcakes*

Mini strawberry cakes

This is a lovely recipe to make with a friend on a summer's day, especially if you can pick your own strawberries from the garden. The frosting is made with squashed strawberries and you should decorate the cakes with the sweetest, juiciest strawberries you can find.

 1 Ask an adult to help you make the cupcakes (see page 8).

2 Cut off the leaves from your two large strawberries, then use a fork to mash them in a bowl until there are no lumps.

3 Add the confectioner's (icing) sugar a little at a time and mix until the frosting is quite smooth. If the mixture is too thick, add another mashed strawberry (which will make the frosting a darker pink) or a few drops of water.

You will need:

1 quantity Vanilla cupcake mix (see page 8)

2 large ripe, juicy, fresh strawberries

1⅓ cups (175 g) confectioner's (icing) sugar

a handful of strawberries, to decorate

12-hole muffin pan, lined with paper cupcake cases

(makes 12)

Who will get the cake with the BIGGEST STRAWBERRY?

4 Spoon the frosting onto the cakes and decorate with sliced or whole strawberries.

Crystallized pansies

These are probably the prettiest cupcakes in the book! They are made with real flowers from your garden, crystallized with egg white and sugar. And they even taste good! You can crystallize rose petals or violets in the same way but don't try other flowers as some are poisonous.

1 The day before you need the cupcakes, pick the fresh pansies from your garden. (Make sure that the flowers are clean and bug-free, and haven't been sprayed with any chemicals.) Leave a short stalk on the pansies so that you can just hold them.

You will need:

1 quantity Vanilla cupcake mix (see page 8)

1 quantity Sugar icing (see page 20)

For the pansies:

fresh pansies (ask before you pick them)

clean salt shaker filled with superfine (caster) sugar

2 eggs

12-hole muffin pan, lined with paper cupcake cases

baking tray lined with baking parchment

fine paintbrush

egg whisk

(makes 12)

2 Line a baking tray with baking parchment and sprinkle some superfine (caster) sugar over it.

3 Ask an adult to help you break the eggs and separate the whites from the yolks (see page 22). Put the egg whites into a medium-sized bowl.

Note: It will take a long time and lots of flowers to make enough crystallized flowers for 12 cakes so just make enough for a few special cupcakes.

4

Add one teaspoon of water to the egg whites and then beat them with an egg whisk until they become frothy.

5

Hold one pansy by its stalk and, using a fine paintbrush, carefully paint the flower, top and bottom, with a thin layer of egg white. Make sure that you cover it all over.

6 Hold the pansy over a shallow bowl and use the salt shaker to sprinkle sugar all over it. The sugar will stick to the egg white. (If you don't have a salt shaker, put the sugar in the bowl and use a dry teaspoon to sprinkle it over the pansy.) Place the sugared pansy onto the lined baking tray to dry. Start the next one.

7 Let the flowers dry in a cool dry place. They will take 12–24 hours to dry and become hard. You can carefully turn them once or twice as they dry to make sure that they dry on all sides.

8 The next day ask an adult to help you make the cupcakes (see page 8). While they are cooling make some sugar icing (see page 20). When the cupcakes are cold, pour a little sugar icing onto each cupcake and spread it to the edges.

9 Use two or three of the crystallized flowers to decorate each cupcake. Serve on a pretty cake plate.

Spotty cupcakes

These spotty cupcakes look very impressive but are quite easy to make. Choose any two colors you like—how about black and white for a "One Hundred and One Dalmatians" themed party?!

1 Ask an adult to help you make the cupcakes and let them cool (see page 8).

You will need:

1 quantity Vanilla cupcake mix (see page 8)

1 lb (500 g) ready-to-roll fondant icing

food coloring in 2 different colors

confectioner's (icing) sugar

2 tablespoons apricot jelly (jam)

12-hole muffin pan, lined with paper cupcake cases

rolling pin

round cookie cutter, 2½ in. (6.5 cm) diameter

round cookie cutter, ¾ in. (1.5 cm) diameter

pastry brush

(makes 12)

2 Tint half of the fondant icing using one color of food coloring (see page 21). Add the paste or liquid a little at a time and knead it until the color is well blended and the shade you want. Tint the other half of the icing with the other color.

3 Sprinkle a little confectioner's (icing) sugar onto a clean work surface. Roll out half of the first color icing until it is about ¼ in. (5 mm) thick and large enough to cut out 3 circles with the large cookie cutter (but don't cut them yet). Each time you roll the icing, lift it, turn it a little, and add more confectioner's sugar to stop it sticking to the work surface. Sprinkle a little confectioner's sugar onto the rolling pin, too, if that sticks. Now roll out half the other color icing to the same size. Put the two sheets of different color icing side by side.

4

Using the smaller cookie cutter, cut circles all over the two sheets of icing. Space each of them about ½ in. (1 cm) apart to create a spotty pattern. Cut the same number of circles on each color icing.

5

Very carefully, without tearing the icing, pick up a circle from one color and swap it with a circle from the other color. Use the tip of a rounded knife to help you lift the circles. Keep doing this until you end up with two spotty sheets of icing.

6

Using the rolling pin, gently roll over the spotty sheets to stick the spots into the icing. Don't push too hard or the spots will change shape.

7

Using the larger cookie cutter, cut out 3 circles from each sheet.

8

Warm the jelly (jam) in a small saucepan or in a bowl in the microwave for 20–30 seconds on medium (see page 22) to melt it and then sieve it into another small bowl to remove any lumps. While it is still warm, use the pastry brush to brush it onto the tops of the cupcakes. The jelly acts as glue.

9

Place a spotty icing circle on top of the jelly and press it down gently.

10

Either roll out the rest of the icing to make plain tops for the other two cakes or, if you have plenty of time, make a second lot of spotty cakes.

Note: These spotty cupcakes take quite a long time to make. We suggest you use half the icing of each color to make six spotty cakes and then you could make six more cakes using plain icing—three in each color. It's up to you.

Spots, SPOTS, spots, SPOTS!

A rainbow of cupcakes

Each of these little cakes is topped with buttercream and a selection of candies and sprinkles in all the colors of the rainbow. Have fun buying and sorting out the candies to match the frosting.

1

Ask an adult to help you make the cupcakes (see page 8). While the cakes are cooling, make one quantity of buttercream frosting.

2

Divide the buttercream between 7 bowls (or however many you need for the colors you're using). Tint each one a different color (see page 21). Tint them the shade you like by very gradually adding more coloring.

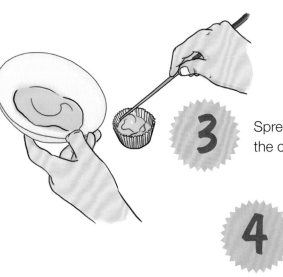

You will need:

1 quantity Vanilla cupcake mix (see page 8)

1 quantity Buttercream frosting (see page 18)

food coloring pastes in rainbow colors—red, orange, yellow, green, blue, indigo, and violet or liquid food colors that you can mix to make more colors

little candies and sprinkles in rainbow colors

12-hole muffin pan, lined with paper cupcake cases

(makes 12)

3

Spread the buttercream over the cold cupcakes.

4

Sort the candies into the different colors and arrange them on the matching cakes.

I can SING a rainbow!

Christmas stockings

Marzipan is great for modeling shapes to decorate cupcakes. This marzipan stocking is a really simple way to decorate a festive cupcake for people who don't like Christmas fruit cake. If they don't like marzipan either, you could use fondant icing instead. Of course, you will be able to think of all sorts of other Christmassy objects to make and pop on top of your cupcake.

You will need:

1 quantity Vanilla cupcake mix (see page 8)

10 oz. (300 g) natural marzipan (or fondant icing if you prefer)

red food coloring paste or liquid

1 quantity Buttercream frosting (see page 18)

red, green, and white sprinkles

12 sugar snowflakes

airtight container lined with baking parchment

12-hole muffin pan, lined with paper cupcake cases

(makes 12)

1 Make the Christmas stockings the day before you make the cupcakes so the color has time to dry. First, find an airtight container to keep your stockings in overnight. Cut a piece of baking parchment to fit the bottom of the box.

2 Tint the marzipan red using the red food coloring (see page 21). Add the paste or liquid a little at a time and knead until the marzipan is bright red. If you are using the liquids, make a hole with your finger in the marzipan and drop in a couple of drops of liquid. Knead the marzipan until the color spreads through it. Gradually add more coloring until you have the red color you want.

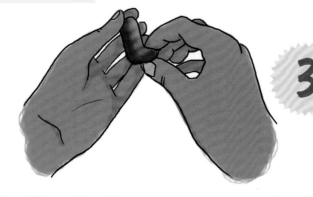

3 Mold the marzipan into 12 Christmas stockings. Put them into the airtight box and let them dry overnight.

4 Ask an adult to help you make the cupcakes (see page 8). While they are cooling, make the buttercream frosting (see page 18). Once the cakes are cold, spread a thick layer of frosting over the top of each cupcake.

5 Mix the red, green, and white sprinkles in a bowl. Dip the edges of the cupcakes into the mixed sprinkles.

6 Top the buttercream with a marzipan stocking. Stick a sugar snowflake onto each stocking with a dab of leftover buttercream.

WHAT ELSE could you make to TOP YOUR CAKE?

Butterfly cakes

A butterfly surprise! A slice of cake forms the butterfly wings and they hide a layer of gorgeous buttercream frosting. You can choose different flavors for the cake and the frosting. Orange or lemon flavors are tangy and delicious.

1 Ask an adult to help you make the cupcakes (see page 8). While the cakes are cooling, make one quantity of buttercream frosting and add whatever flavoring you have chosen (see page 18).

You will need:

1 quantity Vanilla cupcake mix (see page 8)

1 quantity Buttercream frosting (see page 18)

your choice of flavoring (see page 19)

sprinkles

12-hole muffin pan, lined with paper cupcake cases

(makes 12)

2 When the cakes are cool, slice a small disc off the top of each (just the top point—don't cut right to the edge of the cake). Cut this disc in half and put the halves to one side.

3 Cover the circle you have left on the cake with a blob of buttercream frosting.

Butterfly **CAKES THAT WILL FLY** off the plate

4 Push the two halves of cake into the frosting to form the wings of a butterfly. Decorate with sprinkles.

Special name cupcakes

These cupcakes are great for parties. You can use them as place names at the tea table, or let everyone find their own special cupcake on the plate when it comes to dessert. The flags are as fun to make as the cakes.

1 Ask an adult to help you make the cupcakes (see page 8). While the cakes are cooling, make one quantity of buttercream frosting. Add your chosen flavor and color (see pages 19 and 21).

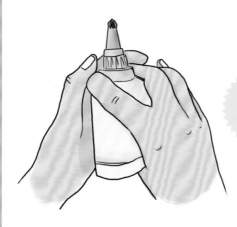

You will need:

- -

1 quantity Vanilla cupcake mix (see page 8)

1 quantity Buttercream frosting (see page 18), flavored if you like (see page 19)

food coloring paste or liquid (choose your favorite color)

colored sprinkles

For the flags:

small piece of stiff card (a cereal packet works well)

thin colored card

glue stick

glitter pen

12 toothpicks

12-hole muffin pan, lined with paper cupcake cases

piping bag, fitted with a star tip

(makes 12)

2 Spoon the frosting into the piping bag. Holding it over the bowl, squeeze the frosting down the bag until it reaches the tip.

3 Now hold it over the first cake and gently squeeze the bag to make a star decoration on the cake. This is quite tricky and needs practice but don't worry if the first ones aren't perfect. Pipe stars all over the cake and remember: even less than perfect cakes will taste good. Sprinkle colored sprinkles over the stars.

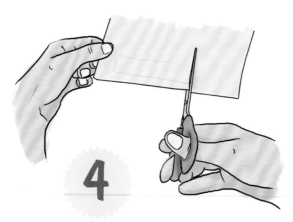

4

To make the flags, draw and cut out a 3 x 1-in. (8 x 2.5 cm) rectangle from the stiff card. Using this as a template to draw round, draw 12 rectangles on the thin card. Cut them out.

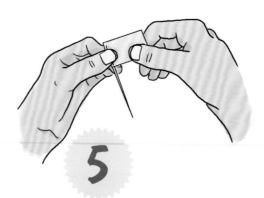

5

Fold each rectangle in half. Spread glue on the inside of one half. Hold a toothpick inside the folded card and glue the two pieces of card together to make a flag. Make up all 12 flags.

6 Snip the flags to turn them into any shape you like.

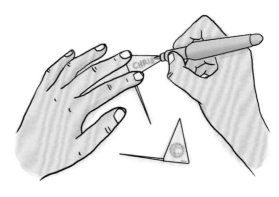

7 Write names on the flags with a glitter pen. Let them dry, then stick the flags into the cakes.

Sparkling diamond cupcakes

If you are having a pirate party, you need treasure; if you're having a princess party, you need jewels. Whatever the party, these diamond cupcakes will add sparkle to your birthday table. You could use different colored hard candies for rubies, emeralds, and sapphires.

You will need:

1 quantity Vanilla cupcake mix (see page 8)

about 6 clear mint candies

1 lime or lemon

1⅓ cups (175 g) confectioner's (icing) sugar

blue food coloring

12-hole muffin pan, lined with silver cupcake cases

rolling pin

lemon squeezer

(makes 12)

1 Ask an adult to help you make the cupcakes (see page 8).

2 While they are cooling, make your "diamonds." Leave the mints in their wrappers. Place them on a chopping board and then tap them with a rolling pin to break them into small pieces. Empty the pieces out of the wrappers onto a small plate.

3 Next, make the lime or lemon-flavored icing. First use the lemon squeezer to squeeze the juice out of the lime or lemon.

A **TREASURE TROVE** of cupcakes

4

Put 2½ tablespoons of juice into a bowl (take out any pips). Place the strainer (sieve) over the bowl and shake the sugar through it into the bowl.

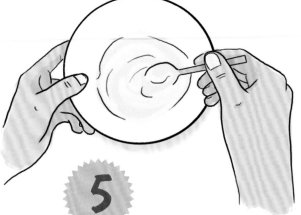

5

Stir the mixture until the icing is smooth with no lumps. Add a few more drops of juice or water if the icing is too thick, but be careful not to make it too runny. Add a llittle more icing sugar if it is too runny. Tint the icing with little blue coloring paste or a few drops of blue food coloring liquid (see page 21) and stir until it is an even color.

6

Spoon the sugar icing onto the cupcakes so that it spreads right to the edges.

7

Pile a little heap of mint "diamonds" on each cupcake.

Pink piggy cupcakes

These cute pink piggies use fondant icing. If you enjoy rolling, cutting, and molding shapes you'll enjoy making these. If you love these pigs, you might like to try the animal cupcakes on page 58 too.

1 Ask an adult to help you make the cupcakes and let them cool (see page 8).

You will need:

1 quantity Vanilla cupcake mix (see page 8)

red food coloring paste or liquid (if coloring the fondant)

1½ lb (750 g) ready-to-roll white or pink fondant icing

confectioner's (icing) sugar

2 tablespoons raspberry jelly (jam)

black writing icing or black food coloring paste

12-hole muffin pan, lined with paper cupcake cases

three round cookie cutters, one about the same size as your cupcake cases, one slightly smaller, and one very small

(makes 12)

2 If you are coloring white fondant, add a little red food coloring to the fondant icing (see page 21) and knead it until the color is well blended and the icing is all pale pink.

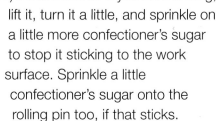

3 Sprinkle a little confectioner's (icing) sugar onto a clean work surface. Roll out the pink icing until it is about ¼ in. (5 mm) thick. Each time you roll the icing, lift it, turn it a little, and sprinkle on a little more confectioner's sugar to stop it sticking to the work surface. Sprinkle a little confectioner's sugar onto the rolling pin too, if that sticks.

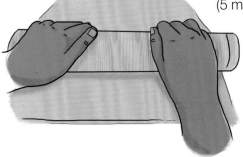

4 Take the largest cookie cutter and stamp out 12 circles.

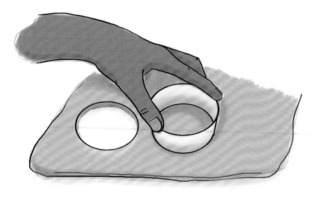

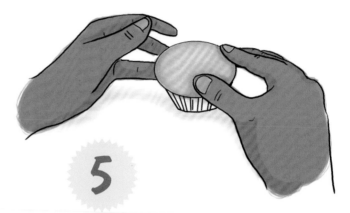

5 Ask an adult to help you warm the jelly (jam) in a small saucepan or in a microwave-safe bowl in the microwave for 20–30 seconds on medium (see page 22), to melt it and then sieve it into another small bowl to get out all the lumps of fruit and pips. While it is still warm, use a pastry brush to brush it onto the tops of the cupcakes. The jelly acts as glue. Gently press the pink circles on top.

6 Gather up all the scraps of icing, knead them together, and then roll out the icing again. This time use the medium-sized cookie cutter to cut out 12 medium circles for the piggies' faces. Brush one side of the circles with water, and stick them onto the cupcakes towards the bottom of the first circle. Press gently in place.

One **LITTLE PIGGY** went to market...

Now with the smallest cutter, stamp out 12 circles of icing (you may need to gather the scraps up again and roll out the icing one more time). Brush one side of each small circle with water and place the circles in the centers of the piggies' faces to make their snouts. Press them gently in place. Using a toothpick, make two round holes in each snout for nostrils.

Using all the scraps of icing you have left, cut out 24 small oval shapes for ears then brush the back of each with water. Fix two in place on top of each piggy's head, turning the tips of the ears up slightly.

Roll a little icing into corkscrew tails and stick on.

You can draw on the mouth and eyes using black writing icing or you can dip the end of a toothpick into black food coloring and use it like a pen.

Victoria cupcakes

These cupcakes have little lids on top of a scrumptious layer of jelly (jam), cream, and strawberries. To make the lids, the cakes need to rise over the height of the paper case, then you can slice the top off—so don't use deep cupcake cases. Go for pretty ones, which are about 1 in. (2.5 cm) deep, and fill them up well with cake mixture.

You will need:

1 quantity Vanilla cupcake mix (see page 8)

strawberry jelly (jam)

¾ cup (175 ml) heavy (whipping) cream

8 oz. (200 g) strawberries

confectioner's (icing) sugar, for dusting

12-hole shallow muffin pan, lined with shallow paper cupcake cases

wire whisk

(makes 12)

1 Ask an adult to help you make the cupcakes (see page 8). Be sure to fill the cases at least three quarters full so they rise above the paper when they cook.

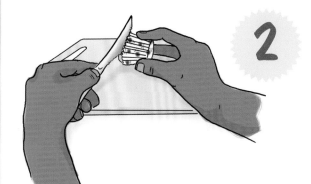

2 When the cakes are cool, using a serrated knife, carefully slice off the tops down to the level of the paper liner.

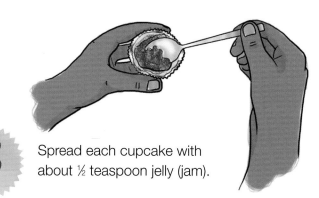

3 Spread each cupcake with about ½ teaspoon jelly (jam).

Strawberry CAKES WITH LIDS on top

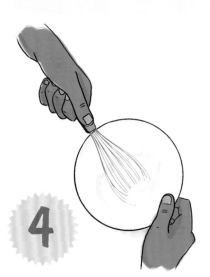

4

Pour the cream into a bowl and beat it with a wire whisk until it is stiff. (An electric beater makes this easier if an adult can help you!) Put a spoonful on top of each of the jelly-covered cakes.

5

Using a sharp knife, carefully cut the strawberries into slices and arrange a few slices on top of the cream on each cake.

6

Top each cake with its lid. Use a strainer (sieve) to dust the tops with confectioner's (icing) sugar.

Princess cupcakes

These cupcakes give you the challenge of using a piping bag, which can be messy and tricky but is lots of fun. And, boys, you don't need to keep to a princess theme or colors!

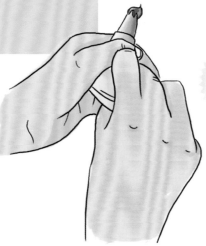

You will need:

----

1 quantity Vanilla cupcake mix (see page 8)

1 quantity Buttercream frosting (see page 18)

food coloring pastes or liquids of your choice

colored sprinkles

12-hole muffin pan, lined with paper cupcake cases

a piping bag, fitted with a star tip

(makes 12)

1 Ask an adult to help you make the cupcakes (see page 8). While the cakes are cooling, make one quantity of buttercream frosting (see page 18).

2 Divide the buttercream between 3 or 4 bowls, depending how many shades of food coloring you are planning to use. Tint each bowl a different color (see page 21).

3 Spoon the frosting from one bowl into the piping bag. Holding it over the bowl, squeeze the frosting down the bag until it reaches the tip.

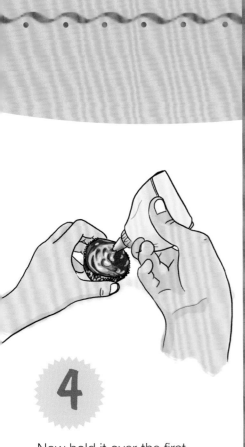

4

Now hold it over the first cake and, gently squeezing the bag, pipe swirls of frosting onto the cake. Try to keep the frosting coming out without breaking off—this is tricky and needs practice, but don't worry if the first ones aren't perfect. Covered with lots of sprinkles they'll look good and taste good too.

5

When you have finished with one color, wash and dry the bag and tip and start on another color.

6

Sprinkle on your sprinkles before the buttercream starts to set.

Animal-face cupcakes

A cat, a monkey, a pig, a bear! What other animal faces could you make out of a cupcake? How about a frog, a panda, or a lion? There is loads of fun to be had making these or other animal faces you have invented yourself.

You will need:

What you need to decorate depends on the animals you are making. You may not need everything.

1 quantity Vanilla cupcake mix (seee page 8)

1 quantity Buttercream frosting (see page 18)

food coloring pastes or liquids in assorted colors

2½ oz. (65 g) bittersweet (dark) chocolate, chopped (if you are making brown animals)

marshmallows in assorted sizes and colors

jelly beans in assorted colors

licorice strips

white, milk, and bittersweet (dark) chocolate buttons in assorted sizes

chocolate and white sprinkles

writing icing

12-hole muffin pan, lined with paper cupcake cases

(makes 12)

1 Ask an adult to help you make the cupcakes (see page 8). While the cakes are cooling, make one quantity of buttercream frosting (see page 18).

2 Decide what animals to make with the decorations you have. Plan them out before you ice the cakes.

3 To make a teddy bear, monkey, or any other brown animal face, put the chocolate in a heatproof bowl and ask an adult to help you set it over a pan of barely simmering water, or melt it in the microwave following the instructions on page 23. Stir until smooth and melted. Put about a third of the buttercream frosting in a bowl and add the melted chocolate. Stir until well mixed.

Make a funny **ANIMAL FACE** for each of your friends!

4 For other color animals, decide what colors you need and divide the buttercream frosting into separate bowls. For example if you wanted pink for pigs, white for rabbits, and green for frogs divide your frosting into 3 bowls. Tint each bowl with a different color (see page 21).

5 Cover the tops of the cold cupcakes with the tinted buttercream, spreading smoothly to the edges with a palette knife.

6 Sprinkle on white or chocolate sprinkles for fur.

7

Use different-sized marshmallows to make noses and snouts. Push a marshmallow into the cupcake and cover it with tinted buttercream to match the rest of the face.

8

You can also cut a large marshmallow in half and pinch or squash with your fingers to shape into ears. Stick them at the top of the cupcake. If you want them to be pink inside, spread a little buttercream on them and sprinkle them with pink sprinkles.

9

Use halved jelly beans for nostrils or large eyes. Strips of licorice positioned under the nose make good mouths or whiskers.

10

Use chocolate buttons for ears. Stick them in place with a dab of buttercream.

11

Draw on smiles or other features with writing icing.

Chocolate and jelly bean cupcakes

Who doesn't like thick chocolate fudge frosting on a cake? This frosting is easy to make. Spread it generously onto your cupcakes and decorate with jelly beans or cake decorations for a real treat.

1 Ask an adult to help you make the chocolate cupcakes (see page 12).

You will need:

1 quantity Chocolate cupcake mix (see page 10)

3½ oz. (100 g) bittersweet (dark) chocolate

1 tablespoon light corn syrup (golden syrup)

2 tablespoons unsalted butter

jelly beans or sprinkles

12-hole muffin pan, lined with paper cupcake cases

(makes 12)

2 While the cupcakes are cooling, make the topping. Break the chocolate up into pieces and put it in a small heatproof bowl with the butter and the corn syrup (golden syrup). Ask an adult to help you set the bowl over a saucepan of gently simmering water, and melt the ingredients together following the instructions on page 23. Take it off the heat and let it cool for 5 minutes. Alternatively, put all the ingredients in a microwave-safe bowl and heat until the ingredients have melted (see page 23). Stir everything together until it is smooth.

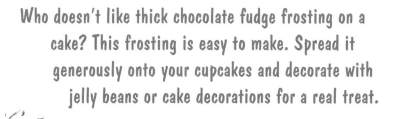

The **BEST CHOCOLATE FUDGE** frosting in town!

3

Let the fudge frosting cool a little before spooning the smooth, runny chocolate on top of the cakes and then add your decoration.

4

Let the topping set before eating (if you can wait!).

"Ice cream" cupcakes

Ice creams that won't melt at your party—this is another fun way to serve cupcakes. You could tint the buttercream pink for strawberry ice cream and then scatter it with fresh strawberries or flavor it with chocolate. You will need to find flat-bottomed cones so that they stand upright for baking. These cakes are best made on the day of the party.

You will need:

10 ice cream cones (with flat bottoms)

1 quantity Vanilla cupcake mix (see page 8)

2 quantities Buttercream frosting (see page 18)

10 chocolate flakes

sprinkles (optional)

12-hole muffin pan

piping bag, fitted with a star tip

(makes 10)

1 Instead of lining the muffin pan with paper cases, stand the ice cream cones in it.

2 Ask an adult to help you make the cupcakes (see page 8). Divide the mixture between the ice cream cones and bake on the middle shelf of the preheated oven for 20–25 minutes until they are golden and a skewer pushed into the middle of the cupcakes comes out clean.

3 Let the cones cool in the muffin pan for 10 minutes before putting them onto a wire cooling rack to cool completely.

4

Make the buttercream frosting (see page 18) and spoon it into the piping bag. Holding it over the bowl, squeeze the frosting down the bag until it reaches the tip.

5

Now hold the piping bag over the first cone and, gently squeezing the bag, pipe big swirls of frosting onto the cake. Try to keep the frosting coming out without breaking off. This is tricky and needs practice, but don't worry if it's not perfect—it will still look and taste good.

6

Finish by gently pushing a chocolate flake into the frosting and cake. Some colored sprinkles would look good, too.

An ice cream that **WON'T MELT!**

Snowmen in scarves

Create a plate of friendly snowmen for a Christmas party. Making carrot noses and coal eyes is a great way of using up marzipan. Use your imagination for all sorts of different ways to decorate your snowmen. Remember, if you use marzipan for the nose, eyes, and mouth, make them the day before you need them and store them in an airtight box.

You will need:

2½ oz. (65 g) natural marzipan

orange food coloring paste or liquid

black food coloring paste or liquid

1 quantity Vanilla cupcake mix (see page 8)

1 quantity Sugar icing (see page 20)

4 cups (300 g) shredded (desiccated) coconut

colored candy-coated chocolate beans

licorice stick, cut into 6 x ½-in. (1-cm) lengths

chocolate buttons

narrow ribbon, cut into 6 x 10-in. (25-cm) lengths

airtight container lined with baking parchment

muffin pan, lined with 6 paper or silver cupcake cases

mini-muffin pan, lined with 6 mini paper or silver cupcake cases

6 toothpicks

(makes 6 snowmen)

1 The day before you need the cakes, make the marzipan noses, mouths, and eyes. Tint three quarters of the marzipan orange using the orange food coloring paste or liquid (see page 21). Add the paste a little at a time. Knead the marzipan until the color spreads through it. Gradually add more coloring until you have the nice carroty orange color you want. Break off 6 small nuggets of marzipan and roll them between your hands to make 6 carrot shapes.

2 Tint the remaining marzipan black using the black food coloring paste or liquid and roll it into tiny balls, allowing roughly 4 for each snowman's mouth and 1 for each eye. Make the balls for the eyes slightly larger than the ones for the mouth. (Do the math—that makes 12 eye balls and 24 mouth balls!) Now let everything dry out overnight on a sheet of baking parchment in an airtight container.

3 The next day, ask an adult to help you make the snowmen cakes: 6 large ones and 6 small ones (see page 8). Let them cool completely on a wire rack. While they are cooling make the sugar icing, keeping it quite thick (see page 20).

4

When the cakes are cold, spread the icing over the tops of the cakes, right to the edges. Before the icing sets, sprinkle all the cakes with shredded (desiccated) coconut.

5

Now use the small cakes to make the snowmen's heads. Press a marzipan carrot nose into the middle of each one and arrange the tiny black marzipan balls as the eyes and mouths.

6

Use the large cupcakes for the snowmen's bodies. Press two candy-coated chocolate drops down the middle of each one to make buttons. Let the icing set firm.

7 To make the hats, dab a tiny amount of icing in the middle of each chocolate button and stick the licorice onto it.

8

When the icing is firm, stand up one of the snowman body cakes on its side, so the buttons run up the tummy (squash it slightly to make a flat base). Carefully push one toothpick through the top of the paper case and into the cake. Leave about ¾ in. (2 cm) sticking out.

9

Now push one of the snowman head cakes onto the toothpick that is sticking out, pushing through the paper case and into the cake. Be sure that the head is the right way up!

10

Tie a ribbon around the snowman's neck and balance a hat on top (a dab of icing will help it stick.) Make up the other 5 snowmen in the same way.

11

Scatter the rest of the shredded (desiccated) coconut over a pretty plate, to make a winter scene, and arrange the snowmen on the plate.

Six FRIENDLY SNOWMEN on a plate!

CHAPTER TWO

CAKE POPS

Sprinkle pops and swirly pops   72

Sailboat pops   74

Goldfish pops   76

Butterfly pops   78

Alien pops   81

Sheep pops   84

Flower pops   86

Sprinkle pops and swirly pops

Rather than a birthday cake, make some pretty cake pops for party fun. These are easy to decorate and, standing in a glass, make a lovely centerpiece for a party tea table.

1 Prepare the cake pops following the recipe on page 12. Remove the cake balls from the freezer and carefully push a lollipop stick into the base of each one.

2 Break the white chocolate into small pieces and put it into a heatproof bowl. Ask an adult to help you melt it, either over a pan of simmering water (see page 23) or in the microwave on low for 1 minute, stirring with a spoon after 40 seconds. Stir the chocolate until all the lumps have dissolved. If you want colored pops, add a few drops of coloring. If you are using candy melts, melt them in the same way as the chocolate, either in the microwave or on the stove.

3 Take one cake pop, holding it by the stick, and dip it into the chocolate/candy melts. Turn the pop so that it is completely covered in coating. Tap the stick on the side of the bowl to remove any excess coating.

You will need

1 quantity Cake pop mix (see page 12)

7 oz. (200 g) white chocolate or colored candy melts

sugar sprinkles

writing icing

20 lollipop sticks

thin pretty ribbon

(makes 20)

Swirls and sprinkles, HEARTS and FLOWERS!

4

If you are making sprinkle pops, shake sugar sprinkles over the pop before the coating sets. Stand it up in a cup to set and start on the next one.

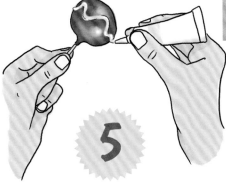

5

If you are making swirly pops, dip the pops in the coating in the same way but stand them up in cups to let them set before you decorate them. When they are set, put some sugar sprinkles in a shallow dish. Now use writing icing to draw thin, wavy lines onto the first pop. Roll it in the sugar sprinkles so that they stick to the icing and then stand the pop in a cup to dry. Start on the next one.

6

Tie a small piece of ribbon onto each stick to decorate.

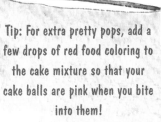

Tip: For extra pretty pops, add a few drops of red food coloring to the cake mixture so that your cake balls are pink when you bite into them!

Sailboat pops

What better end for a seaside picnic or party than to give your guests sailboat pops? With their edible rice paper sails and yummy chocolate hulls, they sail on a sea of blue coconut until it's time to eat them.

You will need:

1 quantity Cake pop mix (see page 12)

2½ cups (200 g) soft, long shredded coconut (such as Baker's Angel Flakes)

5 sheets of thin rice paper

7 oz. (200 g) milk chocolate

blue food coloring

blue and green sugar balls

20 wooden skewers or sticks

(makes 20)

1 Prepare the cake pops following the recipe on page 12, and shape them into small boat shapes. You can do this by making the ball into a teardrop shape and pressing a small hollow into the middle of the boat with your little finger. Put them in the freezer for 30 minutes.

2 Color half of the coconut blue with a few drops of food coloring, mixing it with a fork until it is all colored. Sprinkle the blue coconut and the remaining white coconut together onto a serving plate.

3 On a small piece of cardboard cut out two triangles which you will use as templates for the sails. Draw one about 2 in. (5 cm) high and one 1¼ in. (3 cm) high. Cut them out. Draw round them onto the rice paper so that you have 20 large triangles and 20 small triangles. Cut each of them out and use a cocktail stick or wooden skewer to pierce a hole at the top and bottom of the long straight edge.

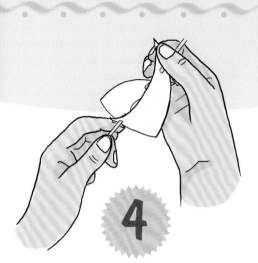

4

Thread one large and one small triangle onto each stick to make the sails. Start by threading the bottom of the large sail onto the stick, then the bottom and top of the small sail and then thread on the top of the large sail last so that the small sail sits in between the top and bottom of the large sail. Put them to one side.

5 Break the chocolate into small pieces and put it into a heatproof bowl. Ask an adult to help you melt it, either over a pan of simmering water (see page 23) or in the microwave on low for 1 minute, stirring after 40 seconds with a spoon. Stir the chocolate until all the lumps have dissolved.

6 Remove the boats from the freezer and push one of the sail sticks into the top of each boat. Dip the boats into the chocolate one at a time. Try not to get any chocolate on the sails. Gently tap the stick on the side of the bowl to remove any excess chocolate.

7 Stand the boats on the coconut and decorate the center of each boat with a few sugar balls. Leave the pops to set.

SAIL AWAY *for a year and a day...*

Goldfish pops

Having a party with a fishy theme? Goldfish pops are a wacky addition to your party tea—create an undersea world for these sweet little fishes to swim through.

You will need

----

1 quantity Cake pop mix (see page 12)

8 oz. (230 g) orange candy melts

black writing icing

small candy drops (optional)

20 lollipop sticks

(makes 20)

1 Prepare the cake pops following the recipe on page 12 and shape them into small fish shapes rather than balls before you put them in the freezer. To do this, take a ball of mixture and roll it into a cylinder shape, then pinch the end between your fingers to make a tail. Put your fishes in the freezer for 30 minutes.

2 Count out 30 candy melts and cut each in half with a knife. These will be used for the fish fins.

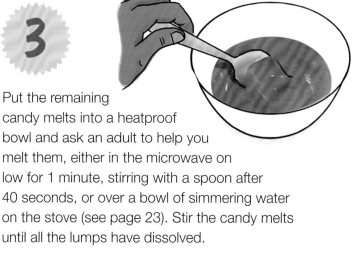

3 Put the remaining candy melts into a heatproof bowl and ask an adult to help you melt them, either in the microwave on low for 1 minute, stirring with a spoon after 40 seconds, or over a bowl of simmering water on the stove (see page 23). Stir the candy melts until all the lumps have dissolved.

Tip: If you prefer, you can make whales using blue candy melts or white chocolate with blue food coloring!

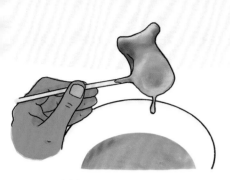

4 Push a lollipop stick into each fish. One at a time, dip the fish into the melted candy, making sure that the fish is completely covered. Stand the pops in cups to let the coating set.

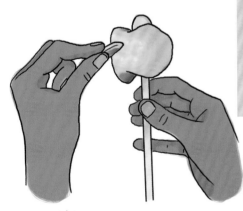

5 Dip the edge of each one of the halved candy melts into the melted candy melts and attach one to either side of the fish and one on top for fins.

6 Draw the eyes on the fish using small dots of writing icing. You can also draw on a mouth or stick on a small candy, by using a little melted candy melt.

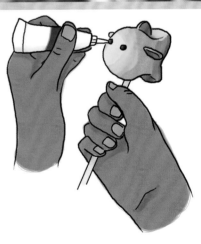

Make **FISHY FRIENDS** for tea!

Butterfly pops

These butterfly pops look as pretty as a picture standing in a bowl of flowers. You could use real flowers or make paper ones and push the stalks and the pop sticks into a ball of modeling clay to hold them firm.

You will need:

- -

Template (see page 126)

1 quantity Cake pop mix (see page 12)

7 oz. (200 g) pink candy melts or white chocolate and pink food coloring

thick edible rice paper

sugar sprinkles and edible silver balls

writing icing

24 lollipop sticks

(makes 24)

1 Prepare the cake pops following the recipe on page 12, shaping them into small tube shapes rather than balls before you put them in the freezer for 30 minutes.

2 Put the candy melts or white chocolate, broken into small pieces, into a heatproof bowl. Ask an adult to help you melt it, either over a pan of simmering water (see page 23) or in the microwave on low for 1 minute, stirring after 40 seconds, with a spoon. Stir until all the lumps have dissolved. If you are using white chocolate, stir a few drops of pink food coloring into the mixture.

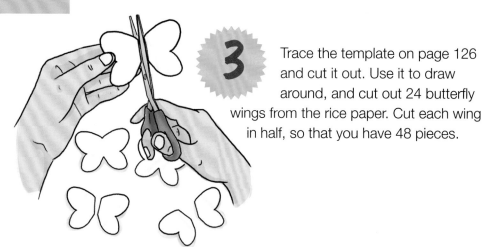

3 Trace the template on page 126 and cut it out. Use it to draw around, and cut out 24 butterfly wings from the rice paper. Cut each wing in half, so that you have 48 pieces.

FLUTTER by, BUTTERFLIES, on your colorful wings!

4 Decorate the wings with the writing icing and stick on sprinkles and silver balls.

5 If you do not have writing icing, you can dip the edge of the wings in a little melted chocolate or candy melts and then dip in the sugar sprinkles to decorate.

6 Remove the pops from the freezer and push a lollipop stick into the base of each one. One at a time, dip the butterfly body in the melted chocolate or candy melts.

7 Stick two matching decorated wings into the coating as it starts to set. Stand the pops in cups to let the coating set.

Alien pops

Weird and wonderful, these alien cake pops will have your friends in fits of giggles. Stick the candy beans in different positions on the chocolate button eyes to give your aliens funny expressions.

You will need:

10 chocolate sticks (such as Matchmakers)

1 quantity Cake pop mix (see page 12)

7 oz. (200 g) blue candy melts or white chocolate and blue food coloring

100 mini candy beans

40 white chocolate buttons

black or brown writing icing

20 lollipop sticks

(makes 20)

1 Ask an adult to help you carefully cut each chocolate stick into 4 pieces for the alien antenna. You should have 40 pieces.

2 Prepare the cake pops following the recipe on page 12. Remove the cake balls from the freezer and carefully push a lollipop stick into the base of each one.

3 Put the candy melts or white chocolate, broken into small pieces, into a heatproof bowl. Ask an adult to help you melt it, either over a pan of simmering water (see page 23) or in the microwave on low for 1 minute, stirring with a spoon after 40 seconds. Stir until all the lumps have dissolved. If you are using white chocolate, stir a few drops of blue food coloring into the mixture until you have a good even blue color.

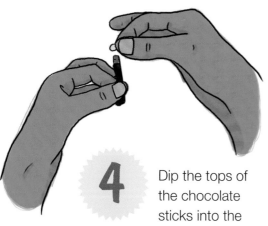

4 Dip the tops of the chocolate sticks into the melted candy melts/chocolate and stick a candy bean on each one. Put these to one side to set while you decorate the aliens.

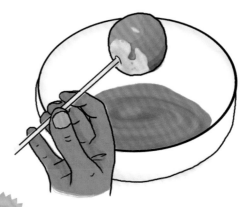

5 Decorate the pops one at a time. Holding the cake pop by the stick, dip it into the chocolate/candy melts, turning the pop so that it is completely covered in coating. Tap the stick on the side of the bowl to remove any excess coating.

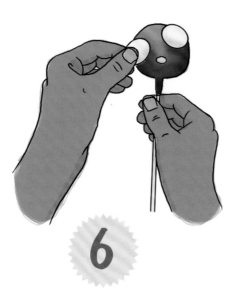

6 Press on two white chocolate buttons for eyes and one candy bean as a nose before the coating sets.

7 For the antennae, dip the end of the sticks without the chocolate bean into the melted candy melts/chocolate and hold in place on top of the alien's head until the coating sets. Attach the second antenna.

BUG-EYED ALIENS *from outer space!*

8 Once the coating has set, lay the alien flat on a piece of greaseproof baking parchment. Stick two candy beans onto the white chocolate buttons using a little of the melted candy melts or chocolate and, if you want, add a small dot of writing icing into the middle of the eyes.

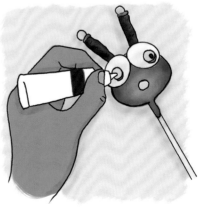

Sheep pops

Who could resist these adorable sheep pops? Covered in tiny marshmallows, they're almost as fluffy as the real thing!

You will need:

1 quantity Cake pop mix (see page 12)

7 oz. (200 g) white chocolate

60 licorice gums or black jelly sweets

mini mini white marshmallows

20 lollipop sticks

(makes 20)

1 Prepare the cake pops following the recipe on page 12. After 30 minutes, remove the cake balls from the freezer and carefully push a lollipop stick into the base of each one.

2 Carefully cut the licorice gums or black jellies into small pieces for the feet and head of each sheep. You need 4 feet and a head for each sheep.

Tip: If you can't find mini mini marshmallows, you can use larger marshmallows and cut them into small pieces using scissors.

3 Break the chocolate into small pieces and put it into a heatproof bowl. Ask an adult to help you melt it, either over a pan of simmering water (see page 23) or in the microwave on low for 1 minute, stirring with a spoon after 40 seconds. Stir the chocolate until all the lumps have dissolved.

MAKE A HERD of cute sheep pops!

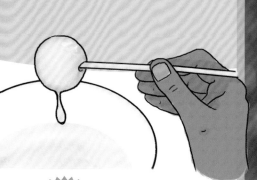

4 Holding the cake pop by the stick, dip it into the melted chocolate, turning the pop so that it is completely covered in coating. Tap the stick on the side of the bowl to remove any excess coating.

5 Decorate one sheep at a time as the chocolate sets quickly. Stick the feet and head to the chocolate.

6 Working quickly, sprinkle the sheep body with the tiny marshmallows. If the chocolate sets before you have added the marshmallows, spoon a little extra chocolate over the body to stick the marshmallows on. Stand the pops in cups to let the coating set.

Flower pops

Three flower pops tied together with a ribbon would make a beautiful Mother's Day gift. With just a few candies arranged carefully in a petal pattern, you can transform a simple cake pop into something really special.

1 Prepare the cake pops following the recipe on page 12, but roll the mixture into balls and then press them flat in your hands to make thick round discs. Put them in the freezer for 30 minutes. Remove the discs from the freezer and carefully push a lollipop stick into the base of each one.

You will need:

1 quantity Cake pop mix (see page 12)

7 oz. (200 g) colored candy melts or white chocolate and food coloring

mini chocolate candy beans

pretty colored candies (such as candy corn, silver dragees, orange and lemon jelly slices)

20 lollipop sticks

(makes 20)

2 Put the candy melts or white chocolate, broken into small pieces, into a heatproof bowl. Ask an adult to help you melt it, either over a pan of simmering water (see page 23) or in the microwave on low for 1 minute, stirring after 40 seconds with a spoon. Stir until all the lumps have dissolved. If you are using white chocolate, stir a few drops of food coloring into the mixture if you like.

3 Decorate the pops one at a time. Holding the cake pop by the stick, dip it into the chocolate/candy melts, turning the pop so that it is completely covered in coating. Tap the stick on the side of the bowl to remove any excess coating.

4 Put a chocolate bean in the center of the pop and position the candies around the outside of the bean to look like petals, before the coating sets. Lay the pop flat on greaseproof baking parchment while the coating sets.

Simple **CANDY PETALS** make colorful flowers!

CHAPTER THREE

BROWNIES, COOKIES, AND GINGERBREAD

Stenciled brownies	90
Rocky roadies	92
Brownie owls	94
Brownie pops	97
Marbled cheesecake brownies	100
Stained glass window cookies	103
Ladybug cookies	106
Christmas tree cookies	111
Witches and wizards	114
Gingerbread family	118
Snowy village	120
Gingerbread animals	124

Stenciled brownies

Stenciling is a great way of decorating rich cakes like brownies that don't need icing. It's quick, easy, and fun. There is a stencil design for these Christmas trees at the back of the book but we have also included a heart and a star for other times of year.

You will need:

1 quantity Brownie mix (see page 14)

confectioner's (icing) sugar, to decorate

For the stencil:

template (see page 127)

a piece of paper (which is a little bigger than one brownie) for the stencil

sharp-pointed scissors

8-in. (20-cm) square baking pan, greased and lined with greased baking parchment

fine-mesh strainer (sieve)

(makes 16)

1

Ask an adult to help you make the brownies (see page 14). When the brownies are completely cold, turn them out of the tin (see page 94, stage 3) and cut them into 16 squares.

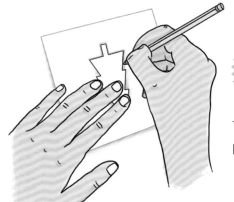

2

Trace the stencil template on page 127 onto the paper.

STENCIL MAGIC—a design for EVERY SEASON!

3

Cut out the stencil shape with a pair of sharp scissors.

4

Take one brownie and hold the stencil over it, carefully positioning the stencil shape in the center of the brownie. Put a spoonful of sugar into the strainer and shake it gently over the paper until the cut out design has a thin layer of sugar all over it. Carefully remove the paper to reveal the stenciled shape— magic! Shake any sugar from the paper back into the strainer and start on the next brownie. Carry on until all the brownies are decorated.

Rocky roadies

This is a feast in one cake—everything you love to eat is piled on top of the rich brownie mix before it is popped back into the oven to melt the chocolate and marshmallows. How good is that? You will need the help of an adult for this one—make sure that they don't eat it all before you can!

1 Ask an adult to help you make the brownies, but bake them for just 20 minutes on the middle shelf of the preheated oven (see page 14).

You will need

1 quantity Brownie mix (see page 14)

1½ cups (75 g) mini-marshmallows

⅔ cup (75 g) chopped walnuts or pecans

¾ cup (100 g) candied (glacé) cherries

½ cup (100 g) bittersweet (dark) chocolate chips

sugar sprinkles

8 x 12-in. (20 x 30-cm) baking pan, greased and lined with greased baking parchment

(makes 16–20)

2 While they are baking, cut the candied (glacé) cherries into small pieces and empty the other ingredients onto small plates ready to use.

3 After 20 minutes, ask the adult to remove the brownies from the oven but don't turn the oven off. Now you need to work quickly. Before the brownies can cool, scatter the marshmallows, nuts, cherries, chocolate chips, and sugar sprinkles evenly over the top to make the Rocky Roadies.

Marshmallows, CHOC CHIPS, cherries, nuts, SPRINKLES... anything else?

4 Ask the adult to put the Rocky Roadies back in the oven for just 3 more minutes or until the marshmallows and chocolate chips are just starting to melt. You can watch them through the window in the oven door, if you have one, but don't get too close.

5 Ask the adult to remove your Rocky Roadies from the oven and let them cool completely in the pan. When they are cool, cut them into rectangles and tuck in. Scrumptious!

Brownie owls

You could make these cute owls in different sizes to create a whole family. You'll find that each owl has a slightly different expression!

1 Ask an adult to help you make the brownies (see page 14) and let them cool completely in the pan. While the brownies are baking, prepare the feathers. Carefully use a sharp knife to slice lots of smaller milk chocolate buttons in half.

You will need:

1 quantity Brownie mix (see page 14)

1 quantity Milk Chocolate Frosting (see page 20)

white and milk chocolate buttons

giant chocolate buttons

chocolate chips

chocolate-covered fudge (or hard caramel) bar

8 x 12-in. (20 x 30-cm) baking pan, greased and lined with greased baking parchment

2½-in. (6–7-cm) round cookie cutter (or different-sized ones for different-sized owls)

(makes 8–10)

2 Make the milk chocolate frosting (see page 20) and while it is thickening, prepare your owls.

3 Loosen around the sides of the pan of brownies with a palette knife. Place a wire rack over the top of the pan and turn it over so that the slab of brownies drops out onto the rack in one piece.

4 Put the slab of brownies onto a board and, using the cookie cutters, stamp out about 8 or 10 round brownies, depending on the size of your cutter.

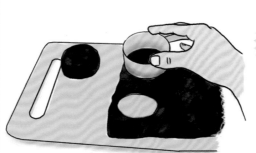

TWIT TWOO, say the brownie owls, TWIT TWOO!

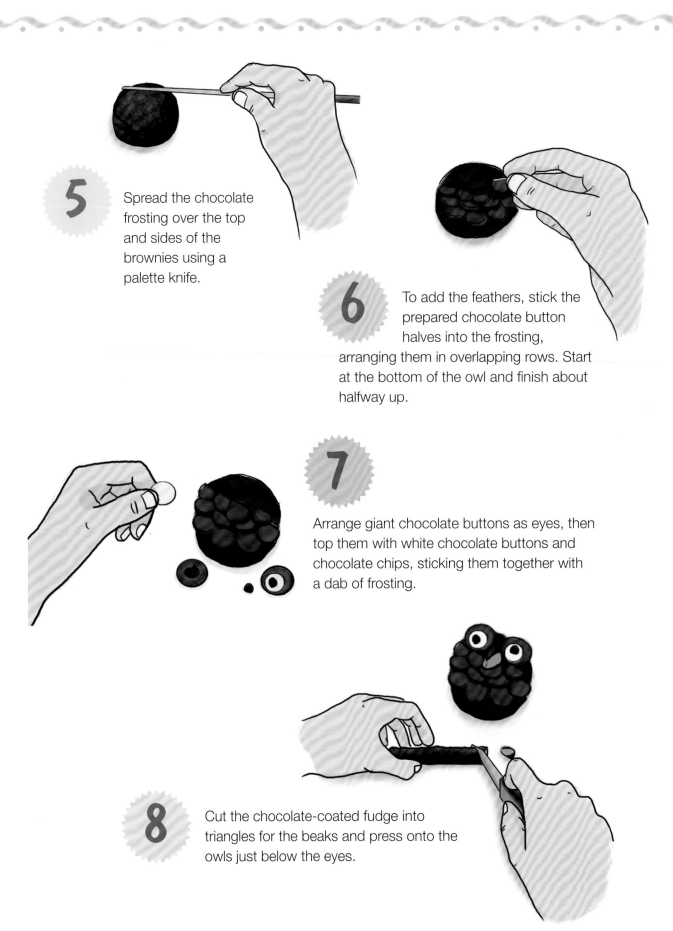

5 Spread the chocolate frosting over the top and sides of the brownies using a palette knife.

6 To add the feathers, stick the prepared chocolate button halves into the frosting, arranging them in overlapping rows. Start at the bottom of the owl and finish about halfway up.

7 Arrange giant chocolate buttons as eyes, then top them with white chocolate buttons and chocolate chips, sticking them together with a dab of frosting.

8 Cut the chocolate-coated fudge into triangles for the beaks and press onto the owls just below the eyes.

Brownie pops

Halfway between a brownie and a lollipop, a brownie pop is a brownie on a stick. Decorate them with different colored sprinkles—these ones have a Christmas theme but you could do whatever you like—what about smiley faces or Valentine's hearts?

You will need:

1 quantity Brownie mix (see page 14)

3–4 tablespoons raspberry or apricot jelly (jam)

1 quantity Milk Chocolate Frosting (see page 20)

assorted sugar sprinkles, stars, candies, etc.

8 x 12-in. (20 x 30-cm) baking pan, greased and lined with greased baking parchment

2-in. (5-cm) round cookie cutter

24 wooden lollipop sticks

pastry brush

baking parchment

(makes 24)

1 Ask an adult to help you make the brownies the day before you plan to decorate them (see page 14). Leave them in the pan overnight so that they are completely cold and won't crumble too much when you cut them.

2 The next day, loosen around the sides of the pan of brownies with a palette knife. Place a wire rack over the top of the pan and turn it over so that the slab of brownies drops out onto the rack in one piece.

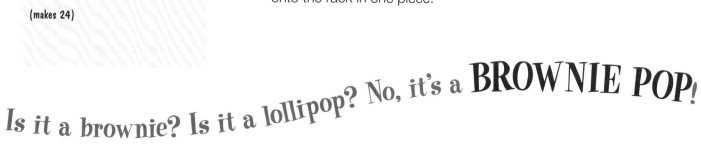

Is it a brownie? Is it a lollipop? No, it's a BROWNIE POP!

3

Put the brownies onto a board and, using the cookie cutter, stamp out 24 round brownies.

4

Carefully push a lollipop stick into each brownie.

5 Warm the jelly (jam) in a small saucepan or in a bowl in the microwave (see page 22) and then sieve it into another small bowl to get out all the lumps of fruit and pips. While it is still warm, use the pastry brush to brush it all over the tops and sides of the brownie pops. Leave them on a wire rack for 5–10 minutes for the jam to cool and set.

6

Meanwhile, prepare the Milk Chocolate Frosting (see page 20) and let it cool and thicken slightly.

7

Using the palette knife, spread the milk chocolate frosting all over the brownie pops. Lay them on a sheet of baking parchment and leave until the frosting is starting to set.

8

Decorate with patterns of sprinkles or candies on the front. Scatter lots of sprinkles on the sides. Serve them standing up in cups so that you don't spoil the decoration!

Marbled cheesecake brownies

This is a very different way to decorate brownies and makes them into a delicious dessert to follow a special meal.

1 Ask an adult to help you make the brownie mixture, leaving out the nuts (see page 14), but don't bake it yet.

You will need:

1 quantity Brownie mix (see page 14), without nuts

For the cheesecake mixture:

1½ cups (350 g) cream cheese

1 teaspoon vanilla extract

⅔ cup (125 g) superfine (caster) sugar

2 eggs, lightly beaten

8 x 12-in. (20 x 30-cm) baking pan, greased and lined with greased baking parchment

(makes 16–20 portions)

2

Now make the cheesecake mixture. Tip all the ingredients into a bowl and beat them together with a wooden spoon until they are smooth.

3 Spoon three-quarters of the brownie mixture into the baking pan and spread it so it's level.

Swirls of **SCRUMMY BROWNIE** and cheesecake!

4 Spoon the cheesecake mixture evenly over the top.

5 Dollop the remaining brownie mixture in spoonfuls over the cheesecake mixture.

6 Using a round-bladed knife, swirl the mixtures together to create a marbled effect. Tap the pan on the work surface to level the mixture.

7 Ask an adult to put the pan on the middle shelf in the oven and bake it for about 30–35 minutes, or until it is just set in the middle.

8 Ask an adult to take the pan out of the oven and let it to cool completely in the pan before turning it out and cutting it into portions to serve.

Stained glass window cookies

This is a lovely way to decorate cookies to hang by a window or on a Christmas tree. You use melted candies in different colors to make the stained glass. The cookies look really magical when light shines through them.

You will need:

1 quantity Gingerbread dough (see page 17)

all-purpose (plain) flour, for rolling out

4½ oz. (125 g) clear, hard, fruit candies

writing icing

narrow ribbon

2 baking trays

nonstick baking parchment

cookie cutters (Christmas ones for Christmas decorations)

small shaped cookie cutters

a drinking straw

plastic freezer bags

pastry brush

(makes 10–12)

1 Ask an adult to help you make the Gingerbread (see page 17). When the dough is well chilled, turn the oven on to 325°F (170°C) Gas 3. Cut pieces of nonstick baking parchment to cover the baking trays.

2 Lightly dust a clean, dry work surface with flour and roll out the dough to ¼ in. (5 mm) thick. Cut cookies from the dough and lay them on the baking trays.

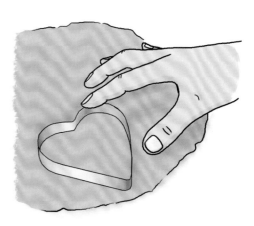

Watch the **LIGHT SHINE** through these beautiful cookies!

3 Cut a hole for the stained glass window in each cookie—either use a smaller cutter or a sharp knife.

4 Use the drinking straw to make a small hole for the ribbon at the top of each cookie.

5 Unwrap the fruit candies, divide them into separate colors, and place each color in its own plastic bag. Using a rolling pin, crush the candies into small pieces and then pour each color into a separate bowl. Put them to one side.

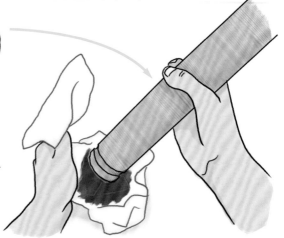

6 Ask an adult to help you bake the cookies on the middle shelf of the preheated oven for about 5 minutes until the gingerbread is just starting to color at the edges. Remove the baking trays from the oven.

7 Carefully and neatly fill the windows in the cookies with the crushed fruit candies. Use a dry pastry brush to brush away any stray candy pieces. Return the baking trays to the oven and bake for 5 more minutes until the gingerbread is golden brown and firm and the candies have melted to fill the window shapes. Be careful not to bake them for too long—if the candies start to bubble they could lose their color.

8

Let the cookies cool completely on the baking trays, then use writing icing to add extra decorations.

9

Finally, thread pieces of ribbon through the holes. Hang your cookies where the light can shine through the colored centers.

stained glass window cookies **105**

Ladybug cookies

These ladybug cookies are a lovely way to brighten up a summer picnic or party. They take quite a long time to make so you could just make a few and stamp out some simple cookie shapes with the rest of your cookie mix. If you can get it, it is much better to use ready-colored fondant icing for these so that you get really bright, strong colors.

You will need:

1 quantity Vanilla cookie dough (see page 16)

confectioner's (icing) sugar

To decorate 6 ladybugs:

5 oz. (150 g) each ready-to-roll black and red fondant icing, or 10 oz. (300 g) white fondant icing and black and red food coloring paste or liquid

1 oz. (25 g) white fondant icing (if using ready-to-roll colored icing)

For the ladybug template:

template (see page 126)

paper

stiff card (a cereal packet works well)

scissors

2 baking trays

nonstick baking parchment

round cookie cutter about 3½ in. (9 cm) diameter

other cookie cutters

(makes 12 cookies)

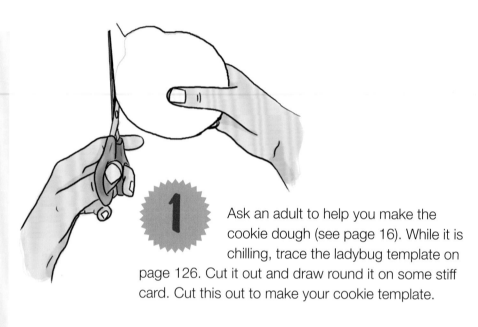

1 Ask an adult to help you make the cookie dough (see page 16). While it is chilling, trace the ladybug template on page 126. Cut it out and draw round it on some stiff card. Cut this out to make your cookie template.

2 Cut some baking parchment to cover your baking trays. Turn the oven on to 400°F (200°C) Gas 6.

3 Sprinkle a clean work surface with flour and roll out the cookie dough until it is about ¼ in. (5 mm) thick.

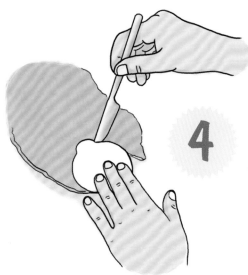

4 Lay the ladybug template on the dough and carefully cut around it with a round-bladed knife. Cut out 5 more in the same way.

5 Use the rest of the dough to stamp out some simple cookie shapes that are about the same size as the ladybugs (so that they take the same time to bake). You will need to gather all the trimmings together and roll them out again.

6 Lay all the cookies on the lined baking trays and ask an adult to put them into the preheated oven for 12–16 minutes, until the cookies are golden. Leave to cool on the baking trays.

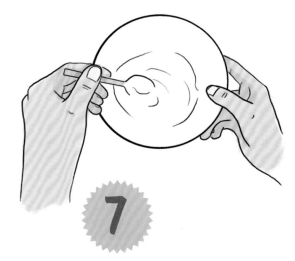

7 Make a little "edible glue" by putting two tablespoons of confectioner's (icing) sugar in a cup and adding two tablespoons of warm water. Stir them together.

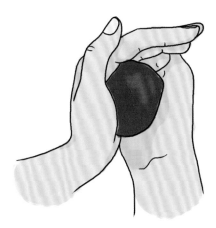

8 If you are coloring your own icing, put a little of the white fondant icing to one side for the ladybugs' eyes. Split the rest in half and color one half black and one half red (see page 21), kneading the icing well to make sure that the color isn't streaky.

9 Sprinkle a little confectioner's (icing) sugar onto a clean work surface. Roll out the black icing until it is about ¼ in. (5 mm) thick. Each time you roll the icing, lift it, turn it a little, and sprinkle on a little more confectioner's sugar to stop it sticking to the work surface. Sprinkle a little confectioner's sugar onto the rolling pin too, if that sticks. Roll out the red icing in the same way.

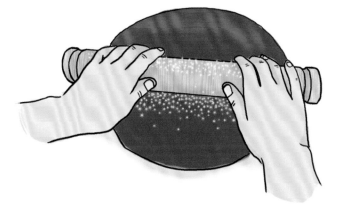

10 Brush a little of your "sugar glue" onto the first cookie.

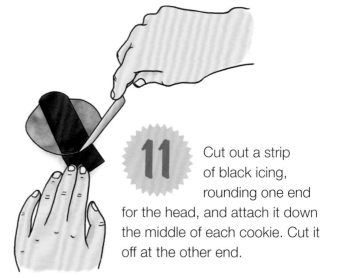

11 Cut out a strip of black icing, rounding one end for the head, and attach it down the middle of each cookie. Cut it off at the other end.

12 Using the large round cookie cutter, cut out a circle of red icing for the wings. Cut it in half to make two wings. Using a little more "sugar glue," attach each of the halves to the cookie joining them in the center by the head.

13 Roll 2 small balls of white icing as eyes. Squash them and stick them to the ladybug (use more "glue"). Add tiny black pupils. Make more black balls, squash them, and stick them on to make spots. Roll a long thin sausage of black icing, to make antennae. You can curl them and put bobbles of icing on the ends if you wish.

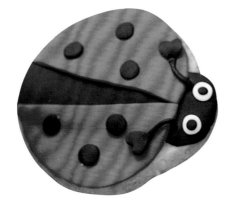

14 Make the other 5 ladybugs in the same way. Use any icing trimmings to decorate your other cookies.

Christmas tree cookies

These yummy cookies, decorated with icing and silver balls, can be threaded with ribbon to hang up on the Christmas tree. They make lovely gifts for teachers or other grown ups.

1 Ask an adult to help you make the gingerbread dough (see page 17). When the dough is well chilled, turn the oven on to 325°F (170°C) Gas 3. Cut pieces of nonstick baking parchment to cover the baking trays.

You will need:

1 quantity Gingerbread dough (see page 17)

all-purpose (plain) flour, for rolling out

writing icing

edible silver balls and other decorations

narrow ribbon

2 baking trays

nonstick baking parchment

a star-shaped cookie cutter

a drinking straw

(makes 25)

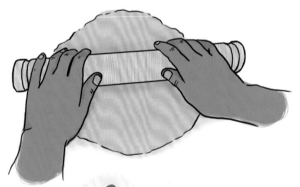

2 Lightly dust a clean, dry work surface with flour and roll out the dough to ¼ in. (5 mm) thick. Using the star cookie cutter, cut cookies from the dough and lay them on the baking trays.

3 Gather the dough scraps together, knead lightly, re-roll, and stamp out more cookies until all the dough has been used up.

4

Use a drinking straw to punch a small hanging hole in each cookie, about ½ in. (1 cm) from the edge.

5

Ask an adult to help you bake the gingerbread in batches on the middle shelf of the preheated oven for 8–10 minutes or until they are firm and lightly browned at the edges.

Leave the baked cookies on the trays for a few minutes, then transfer to a rack to cool.

6

Decorate with writing icing. Stick silver balls or other decorations onto the icing.

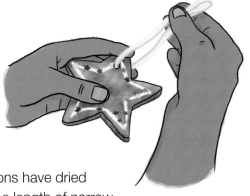

7

Once the decorations have dried completely, thread a length of narrow ribbon through the hole in each cookie and hang them on the Christmas tree.

How long will these **DECORATIONS** last
ON YOUR TREE before you eat them?

Witches and wizards

Are you having a Halloween party, or perhaps a Harry Potter party? These witch and wizard hats would look great on your party table. Like the ladybugs, these hats take quite a long time to make, so you could always use some cookie cutters to make other cookie shapes with half of the dough and icing. You need really black icing for these so it is best to buy ready-colored fondant icing.

You will need:

----

1 quantity Vanilla cookie dough (see page 16)

all-purpose (plain) flour, for rolling out

confectioner's (icing) sugar

2 oz. (50 g) white fondant icing

purple food coloring paste or red and blue food colouring liquids

8 oz. (250 g) ready-to-roll black fondant icing

writing icing in different colors

For the templates:

templates (see page 126)

paper

stiff card (a cereal packet works well)

scissors

2 baking trays

nonstick baking parchment

(makes 12)

1 Ask an adult to help you make the cookie dough (see page 16). While it is chilling, trace the witch and wizard hat templates on page 126. Cut it out and draw round them on some stiff card. Cut these out to make your cookie templates.

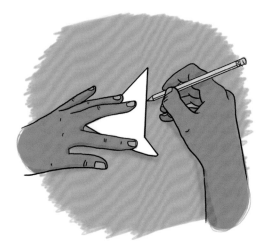

2 Cut some baking parchment to cover your baking trays. Turn the oven on to 400°F (200°C) Gas 6.

3 Sprinkle a clean work surface with flour and roll out the cookie dough until it is about ¼ in. (5 mm) thick.

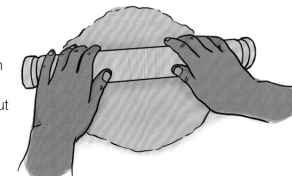

8

Use white writing icing to draw lines and dots around the windows and walls of each house. Draw tiles on the roofs.

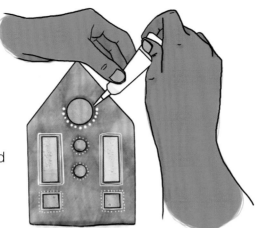

9 Lean the houses up against a window so that the light shines through the "stained glass."

Gingerbread animals

This is the simplest way to decorate cookies—cut out shapes and sprinkle on decorations—an ideal project if you haven't much time or are just a beginner at cake decorating.

1 Ask an adult to help you make the gingerbread (see page 17). When the dough is well chilled, turn the oven on to 325°F (170°C) Gas 3. Cut pieces of nonstick baking parchment to cover the baking trays.

You will need:

1 quantity Gingerbread dough (see page 17)

all-purpose (plain) flour, for rolling out

confectioner's (icing) sugar

colored sugar and candy shots, to decorate

2 baking trays

nonstick baking parchment

animal cookie cutters

(makes 25 cookies)

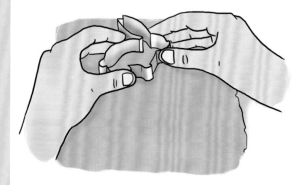

2 Lightly dust a clean, dry work surface with flour and roll out the dough to ¼ in. (5 mm) thick. Using animal cookie cutters, cut cookies from the dough and lay them on the baking trays.

3 Gather the dough scraps together, knead lightly, re-roll, and stamp out more cookies until all the dough has been used up.

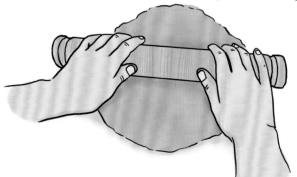

4 Ask an adult to help you bake the gingerbread in batches on the middle shelf of the preheated oven for 8–10 minutes or until they are firm and lightly browned at the edges.

Let the cookies cool completely on the baking trays before icing.

5 To decorate the cookies, beat 2 tablespoons confectioner's (icing) sugar with a teaspoon of water. Add more water a few drops at a time until you have a thin icing. Brush this over the top of the cookies and sprinkle with candy shots or colored sugar.

We're all GOING TO THE ZOO tomorrow!

Templates

All of these templates are full-size templates, so you can trace them off the page to use them.

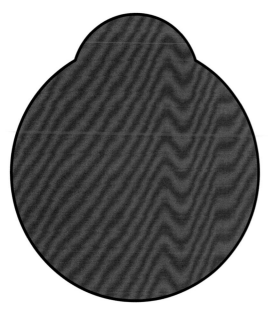

Ladybug cookie (page 106)

Butterfly pops (page 78)

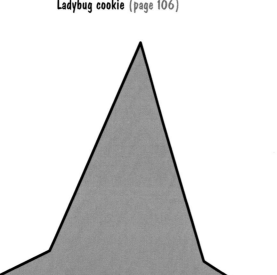

Witches and Wizards (witch's hat) (page 114)

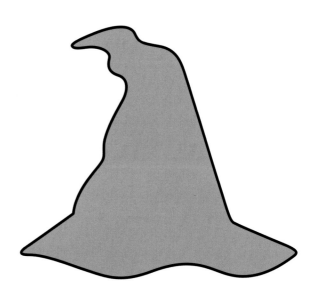

Witches and Wizards (wizard's hat) (page 114)

Stenciled brownies (page 90)

Stenciled brownies (page 90)

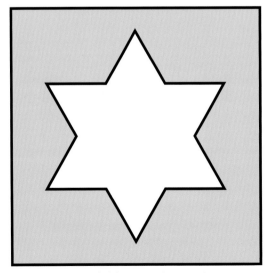

Stenciled brownies (page 90)

Suppliers

Most of the projects in this book use ingredients and materials that you will already have in the kitchen or can buy at the supermarket, but for more specialist cake-decorating ingredients, you can try the following suppliers:

US SUPPLIERS

Cake Art
www.cakeart.com

Fancy Flours Inc
www.fancyflours.com

Global Sugar Art
www.globalsugarart.com

Kitchen Krafts
www.kitchenkrafts.com

Michaels
www.michaels.com

Sugarcraft
www.sugarcraft.com

Wilton
www.wilton.com

UK SUPPLIERS

Cakes, Cookies & Crafts
www.cakescookiesandcraftsshop.co.uk

Hobbycraft
www.hobbycraft.co.uk

John Lewis
www.johnlewis.com

Lakeland
www.lakeland.co.uk

Make a Wish Cake Shop
www.makeawishcakeshop.co.uk

Squires Kitchen
www.squires-shop.com

Sugarshack
www.sugarshack.co.uk

Index

alien pops 81–3
animal face cupcakes 58–61
animals, gingerbread 124–5

basic recipes 8–18
brownie pops 97–9
brownies 14–15
    marbled cheesecake 100–2
    owls 94–6
    rocky roadies 92–3
    stenciled 90–1
buttercream frosting 18–19
    tinting 21
butterfly cakes 42–3
butterfly pops 78–80, 126

cake pops, basic 12–13
    brownie 97–9
    decorated 72–87
candies, hard 47, 103, 120
chocolate, melting 23
chocolate cupcakes 10–11
    with jelly beans 62–3
Christmas stockings 40–1
Christmas tree cookies 111–13
colors, mixing 21
cookie dough 16, 17–18, 106
crystallized pansies 32–4

Easter bunny cupcakes 26–9
eggs, breaking and separating 22

equipment 7

flags 46
flavorings, for frostings 19
flower pops 86–7
fondant icing 19–20, 50–3, 106
frostings and icings 18–21

gingerbread animals 124–5
gingerbread dough 17–18
    Christmas tree cookies 111–13
    snowy village 120–3
    stained glass window cookies
        103–5
gingerbread family 118–19
goldfish pops 76–7

Halloween 114–17

"ice cream" cupcakes 64–5

jelly beans 62–3
jelly, warming 22

ladybug cookies 106–10, 126

marbled cheesecake brownies
    100–2
marzipan 26–7, 40–1, 66
microwave 22, 23
milk chocolate frosting 20

owls, brownie 94–6

pink piggy cupcakes 50–3
princess cupcakes 56–7

rainbow of cupcakes 38–9
rocky roadies 92–3

safety in the kitchen 7, 23
sailboat pops 74–5
sheep pops 84–5
snowmen in scarves 66–9
snowy village 120–3
sparkling diamond cupcakes 47–9
special name cupcakes 44–6
spotty cupcakes 35–7
sprinkle pops 72–3
stained glass window cookies 103–5
stenciled brownies 90–1, 127
strawberries, mini cakes 30–1
sugar icing 20, 21
swirly pops 72–3

templates 126–7
tinting icing 21

vanilla cupcakes 8–9
Victoria cupcakes 54–5

witches and wizards cookies
    114–17, 126

Acknowledgments

Key: l = left, r = right, t = top, b = bottom, c =center

RECIPES Susannah Blake: pages 35–37, 44–46, 47–49, 50–53, 54–55 Chloe Coker: pages 16, 106–110, 114–117 Linda Collister: pages 10–11, 62–63 Amanda Grant: pages 30–31 Caroline Marson: pages 18–19, 20t, 42–43, 124–125 Hannah Miles: pages 14, 72–73, 74–75, 76–77, 78–80, 81–83, 84–85, 86–87 Annie Rigg: pages 8–9, 14–15, 17, 20b, 26–29, 38–39, 40–41, 56–57, 58–61, 64–65, 66–69, 92–93, 94–96, 97–99, 100–102, 118–119, 120–123 Nicki Trench: 103–105 Catherine Woram/Martyn Cox: pages 32–34 Catherine Woram: pages 90–91, 111–113

PHOTOGRAPHY Martin Brigdale: pages 1, 24, 35, 37, 45, 47, 49, 51, 55 Laura Edwards: pages 5t, 89, 93, 95, 97, 99, 101 Tara Fisher: pages 31, 119, 121, 122–123 Winfried Heinze: pages 5c, 103, 105 Sandra Lane: pages 2, 5bl, 57, 65 Emma Mitchell: pages 3, 7, 70–87 Martin Norris: pages 6, 88, 107, 109, 110, 115, 117 Kate Whitaker: pages 4, 5br, 25, 27, 39, 41, 59, 61, 67 Polly Wreford: pages 11, 33, 34, 43, 63, 91, 111, 113, 125

STYLING Liz Belton: pages 2, 5t, 5bl, 57, 65, 89, 93, 95, 97, 99, 101, 119, 121, 122–123 Chloe Coker/Luis Peral-Aranda: pages 3, 7, 70–87 Amanda Grant: pages 30 Rose Hammick: pages 43, 125 Joss Herd/Helen Trent: pages 11, 63, Penny Markham: pages 4, 5br, 25, 27, 39, 41, 59, 61, 67 Luis Peral-Aranda: pages 6, 88, 107, 109, 110, 115, 117 Sue Rowlands/Rose Hammick: pages 5c, 103, 105 Linda Tubby/Helen Trent: pages 1, 24, 35, 37, 45, 47, 49, 51, 55 Catherine Woram: pages 91, 111, 113